Wild Goose Winter

Observations of geese
in north Norfolk

James McCallum

James McCallum.

Silver Brant

© James McCallum 2001

Published by Silver Brant

Corner Cottage
Jolly Sailor Yard
Wells-next-the-Sea
Norfolk
NR23 1LB

ISBN 0-9541695-0-6

Designed by John Walters
www.johnwalters.co.uk

Printed by Healeys Printers
Ipswich 01473 461122

Wild Goose Winter

Observations of geese
in north Norfolk

James McCallum

Pinkfeet coming in to roost, Brancaster - January 2001.

Preface

Wild geese are a dominant feature of the north Norfolk winter landscape. Few could have failed to notice the beautiful charcoal and white Brent Geese with their soft muttering calls in and around the harbours, estuaries and adjoining marshes, or the awe-inspiring, vast noisy skeins of Pink-footed Geese, flighting at dusk to their night time roosts on intertidal sands and mudflats. There are however various other geese which are regularly seen within the area and several more still which are seen only occasionally. Being large birds favouring open terrain, their complex lives, daily routines and remarkably ordered flocks are, with a little time and patience, relatively easy and fascinating to observe.

In this book I have tried to put across as much information in the form of drawings and paintings with short texts written in an informal manner. The observations have been made locally from many years of watching geese and hundreds of hours spent sketching and painting 'in the field'.
Sometimes we can be too quick to take the present day numbers of geese for granted: or, if new to the area, assume that the current situation has always been so.

However, it is worth reminding ourselves that, for Pink-footed and Brent Geese, our two most numerous species, the situation was sadly profoundly different in surprisingly recent decades. Fortunately today these two species winter here in their highest ever recorded numbers.

With so much pressure on our native wildlife and habitats, it is perhaps not surprising, but nonetheless refreshing, to see a large swing in local opinion over the last few years, from geese being seen as farmland pests to a much thought of spectacle, a symbol of wildlife thriving and hope for the future.

Shortly after leaving the roost the geese begin to arrive on their feeding areas in the early morning. They glide and bank into the wind using their body mass, the surface-area of wings and tail and even their feet to reduce the airflow before they flap to land gently. As the geese bank round into the wind, the airflow causes the feathers of their outer wings to lift - 6 January 2000.

Foreword

The table was strewn with the drawings and paintings for this book. We were poring over the mock-up, discussing the positioning of drawings and content of the writing, when James looked up. "Pinkfeet!" We went straight out into the garden in near darkness, to listen to the magical music of the geese beyond the screen of trees to the south. It was mid-September and James had been telling me that Pink-footed Geese had already arrived early at Holkham.

The distant *wink-wink* calls of the Pinkfeet immediately took me back 47 years, to central Iceland, at exactly the same time of year. With my companion, even more of a goose enthusiast than I, we had been watching local Pinks, augmented by Barnacle Geese and other Pinkfeet from Greenland. They were gathering into flocks along the river valley below the Hofsjökull icecap, preparatory to leaving on their non-stop flight to Scotland. Heavy, unseasonal snows were covering their feeding grounds, and the geese flew up and down the valley seeking clear areas. The snow continued and we watched the geese gain height and depart south, knowing they would not stop until they reached the shores of their winter quarters. They left us to get out as best we could – another story.

As schoolboys, geese were our passion. Our hero, Peter Scott, had just started the Wildfowl Trust, and I became a member in its second year. The only geese we had locally were Canadas, a small population breeding on islands in a lake in a private park, within cycling distance of our school in Reading. Nick was the scientist and he led our studies, as the geese began to move out and colonise the chain of gravel pits being excavated along the Kennet Valley. We recorded their increasing numbers and, during the August moults, caught them to put rings on their legs and dye their vents yellow so that we could follow them more easily during the winter. Then, at the end of schooling and before University, we used a Travel Scholarship to find the truly wild geese in Iceland. From university we launched further expeditions to Iceland and Spitsbergen in search of geese. Coming to live in north Norfolk has rekindled that interest and enthusiasm for the great congregations of geese which winter here, so wonderfully described and illustrated in this book.

Over the last decade I have watched James McCallum's development as an artist with admiration and awe. In 1994 I was one of the judges of the annual Bird Illustrator of the Year awards, promoted by the monthly magazine *British Birds*. We presented James with the PJC Award, given for a drawing which "particularly catches the judges' attention for some outstanding quality." At the time I wrote: "We were particularly attracted by one batch of drawings, clearly based directly on material in the artist's sketchbook. We chose one of these...".

It is still this immediacy that attracts me to James's art and I am full of admiration for his method of working. All the drawings in this book were produced in the field, outdoors in all weathers. The wind may tear at the page, the water may freeze in the container and the rain may leave tell-tale marks in the watercolour washes, but James' drive and enthusiasm to record all that he is seeing defies the conditions. Consequently he is able to describe, in words and pictures, what it is like for the geese here in winter. How these intensely social animals behave, react and care for themselves, their families and their flock. In James McCallum the geese have a worthy champion and spokesman, one who explains and interprets their behaviour, imparting a huge fund of knowledge with a lightness and clarity reflected in the accompanying drawings. It is knowledge that has been gained over long periods spent alongside the geese, noting every aspect of their lives.

His eye and his pencil, with lightening speed, catch the essence of his quarry, the character and the jizz of the birds. These drawings are full of life, energy and vitality, as James conjures movement on the page. His birds fly, preen, chase and bathe and are sometimes motionless, alert or asleep, but always very much alive. The colour washes capture the colour and tone of Norfolk in winter, the cold grey skies, the warm brown earth and the similar colours of the geese which often merge them beautifully into their background.

So here we have direct, first-hand observations, in word and line, of the wild geese which make this coastal area of Norfolk so exciting to visit in winter. James' text adds illumination to the experience and I, for one, am very grateful for this.

Robert Gillmor Cley-next-the-Sea September 2001

Low tide in Wells Harbour on a bright cold day with Brent Geese facing a strong south-west wind - 27 February 2001.

Introduction

North Norfolk is one of the premier areas for wintering wild geese in the British Isles and, for two species, the Dark-bellied Brent and the Pink-footed Goose, amongst the most important wintering areas in the world.

This book will focus mainly on the three traditional wintering species, Dark-bellied Brent, Pink-footed and White-fronted Geese, but will also look at regularly observed species such as Barnacle and Bean Geese, as well as unusual visitors and vagrants like Red-breasted and Snow Geese which occasionally arrive with the regular species.

The resident populations of Greylag, Canadian and Egyptian Geese, although very much a part of the local avifauna fall outside the scope of this book. They are, however, briefly mentioned and illustrated for the sake of completeness and to aid identification of the wild visitors.

Pinkfeet arriving on the grazing marshes at Holkham from their night-time roost on the sands east of Wells Harbour mouth. The early morning frost is illuminated by the first rays of the rising sun - November 1998.

A Day in the Life of Winter Geese

To reach our winter shores wild geese undertake migrations of fantastic distances from as far afield as northern Siberia and Iceland. The combination of relatively mild winters and suitable feeding areas has, over the ages, resulted in our coast becoming traditional wintering areas for wild geese.

On arrival here, the basic requirement is a safe, undisturbed roost site to spend the night. This is the first of several needs which we will now explore in greater detail.

Roosting and the roost site

Night time spells potential danger for geese. Staying on their ever-changing and therefore relatively unfamiliar daytime feeding grounds they feel vulnerable to disturbance by man or from attacks by predators such as foxes. Any disturbance would send the geese flying into a dark landscape unknown to them. Instead, geese of the same species gather in large groups as dusk approaches and flight to a traditional or favoured night-time roost, each species having its own special areas at various locations along the north Norfolk coast.

Essential components of these roosts are large open areas of fresh or salt water and vast areas of tidal sands and mudflats, all of which must be free from disturbance. These various locations will be used very frequently, if not nightly, by the different species. The geese use them year after year and become very familiar with the area; they feel more relaxed and more able to move within them if danger should occur unexpectedly. Open water gives good protection from ground predators, whereas vast intertidal flats give geese the option to move quickly to other inaccessible areas and of course, the open sea is never far away.

In the more abundant species, the Pink-footed Goose in particular, the sheer numbers, calls and shape of the skeins moving between feeding areas and roost, against an endless variety of dawn and dusk skies, are one of the wonders of the natural world.

Feeding areas

The distance geese travel from their roosts to their feeding areas can vary quite dramatically. For example, the White-fronted Geese at Holkham and some flocks of Brent Geese may travel under a mile. Other Brent Geese may journey a mile or so; occasionally some flocks travel over six miles. None of the other geese, however, challenge Pinkfeet for the distance, travelled to feed. These distances are related to the abundance of food in those areas in which the flocks feel at ease feeding in.

Pinkfeet favour sugar-beet tops which are left over after the roots have been harvested. They are quite wary and fickle about which fields they feel comfortable feeding in and, therefore, may have to journey a considerable distance to newly-harvested fields.

Pinkfeet skeins over Brancaster - January 2001.

For example, Pinkfeet from the roost at Wells/Warham can travel up to twelve miles to reach their inland feeding areas; not only this, on days when they are repeatedly disturbed, they may fly a further nine miles to reach the relative safety of Holkham grazing marshes. From here they may fly back to inspect their chosen feeding fields. If these remain disturbed the Pinkfeet may return to Holkham, or move on to find suitable feeding areas in the Burnham area, or even Brancaster, and possibly spend the night at another roost site, Scolt Head Island. This to-ing and fro-ing can result in a day's flying of almost sixty miles.

Although acknowledged long-distance migrants, several days of this disturbance would put considerable strain on the geese. Fortunately many Pinkfeet spend their winter days in the main undisturbed, with many favoured feeding areas being roughly between four and seven miles from the roosts. This, combined with perhaps a brief trip to coastal grazing fields at Holkham for a quick bathe, would result in a days flying of around twenty miles.

Our winter geese are best described as vegetarians. They obtain their food by grazing, which describes the manner of feeding by nibbling or tearing vegetation. More details of feeding and food items will be discussed under the individual species' accounts.

Feeding takes place throughout the daylight hours, although there may be a period of less intensive feeding around the middle of the day. At this time there is sometimes even an inactive period with groups dozing for a while.

White-fronted Geese grazing.

Moonlight feeding

It is surprising how many 'daytime' birds are active and feed during the brightest phases of the moon. Whitefronts and especially Pinkfeet are no exception. Brents however seem to be indifferent and stay on the roost. Frequently you can hear them calling and see them lightly picking around on the roost; you are, however, just as likely to see groups sleeping. The Whitefronts' favourite fields are next to the roost so they do not need to travel far and can be heard calling all night, and occasionally, their dark shapes can be made out in the fields. Pinkfeet are another matter and there are few birds that sum up this night time activity as vividly as these geese. During three-quarter or full moonlit nights, skeins of Pinkfeet flight backwards and forwards from roost to feeding areas throughout the night. By choosing a night with patches of high thin cloud which can give the sky a paler, greyer cast you can watch the skeins passing along the night sky and, at lucky moments, across the face of the moon. If the conditions are right, such nights can be among the highlights of a winter's goose watching. It is interesting to observe Pinkfeet the following morning, sluggish and reluctant to leave the roost, or to see large groups sleeping on nearby sugar-beet or cereal fields.

These Brents are conserving energy by sleeping facing the strong, cold wind. As with all flocks there is always at least one eye open looking out for potential danger -21 February 2001.

The moon illuminates high, thin cloud allowing the progress of Pinkfeet to be seen as they head inland to feed. The distinctive trio of stars that makes Orion's belt are briefly visible between clouds - 8 January 2001.

The Flock

Geese are social birds, famous for their gregarious habits, especially during migration and outside the nesting season. On the breeding grounds flocks break up in the sense that a small area around the nest site is vigorously defended; they are however, still frequently found nesting in loose colonies. Soon after the nesting season geese begin to form social groups, which are the beginnings of the large flocks we observe in north Norfolk during the winter. Despite the initial random appearance of these frequently large gatherings, it is clear, after only a short period of observation, that there are certain levels of order within the flock. After more time we can begin to recognise regular patterns of posturing and other behaviour and to understand that there is considerable order and a fascinating social language within the flocks.

The Pair

Not long after watching a group of geese, a bond between two individuals quickly becomes apparent. Many geese seem to be in pairs; this is noticeable by their togetherness and progress together as they move within the feeding flock. With a little experience it is often possible to make out that one of the pair is slightly bulkier and heavier necked than its companion. This is the male, the gander, who has a habit of standing more upright with his head held high, showing off his bulk to nearby birds. This posturing is part of the gander's

A pair of Pinkfeet together on a discarded sugar-beet root.

showing off his readiness to protect his mate and helps to strengthen the pair bond. Geese usually form strong pairs after their first few years and will go on to pair for life. Individual geese, recognised by distinctive markings, are known to be at least twenty years old, so therefore could have been together for at least sixteen years.

An example of a strong pair bond is shown by Pinkfeet when one of a pair is killed by wildfowling on leaving the roost. During the whole of the rest of the day and often longer, the remaining goose will continually fly backwards and forwards to the roost and other familiar areas, calling constantly, in the vain hope that its mate will return its call.

When we appreciate the strong pair bond it is not surprising that the pair will react to any other geese that pass too close to either mate. Threat postures are adopted which, although similar to the gander's upright posturing, vary in intensity and are indicated by the angle of the neck: upright signifies a very mild warning, diagonal a stronger one, with the extreme being neck straight out in front or even slightly downwards with the head tilted up. The threat posture often fluctuates between diagonal and head out forwards. If the offending goose does not react to these signals then a forward run with neck out, angled slightly downwards and head tilted up will follow.

The pair threaten another goose which has passed too closely.

Sometimes in Pinkfeet and Whitefronts this posture will be exaggerated by lifting both wings clear of the back, which, seen from the front gives the body a considerably larger appearance. Brent Geese on the other hand open their bills, displaying a thick, pale pink tongue during stronger threats. These displays are essentially silent threats but in Pinkfeet strange mechanical churring noises are frequently heard when several birds are involved in a heated dispute. Occasionally two pairs will hold their ground and both posture at each other for a while. However, eventually one side will give in. It is extremely rare indeed that an actual fight breaks out.

Parents, like these Brent Geese, threaten another that has come too close to their offspring. Frequently young birds will also join in the threat.

10

To avoid contact, a threatened bird will mainly adopt a submissive posture, keeping its body low, hanging its head and moving a respectful distance away before commencing feeding. Following a confrontation, the victorious goose or pair, in particular the gander, may celebrate its victory by standing tall with neck erect, then flap the wings quickly and hold them spread open for a second or two before closing them. In Pinkfeet and Whitefronts an exaggerated, ritualized form of this can be seen very occasionally after a heated display of threats or after rare conflict between two ganders. The victor, close to his mate, postures by standing tall with wings fully spread and neck and head bent down to touch his chest. This rarely seen triumph display often appears to take place between two quite dominant ganders and brings us to another topic, the idea of a ranking order of dominance within the flock. There is absolutely no doubt of there being a hierarchy of dominance within the winter flocks. Dominant pairs, or at least ganders, are very obvious in the way they posture. These ganders frequently stand taller and appear more confident, with their bills held slightly upwards. They pose like this for quite long periods among the feeding flocks and most other geese keep a respectful distance. The full extent of the hierarchy is difficult to assess due to the ever-changing movements and locations of the geese flocks.

Victory pose.

Geese not only threaten other geese that pass too closely but other birds too. I have watched Pinkfeet seeing off Pheasants and Woodpigeons and in this instance a Jackdaw is moved on - 6 December 2000.

Family Groups

After a successful breeding year some pairs can be seen with young. These families usually begin to arrive several weeks after the first returning geese, as their progress from the breeding grounds will be a little slower. The tight family unit and the parent's protection of it are very evident within the flock. Often the family will feed on the outskirts, or in less dense areas of the flock. In such situations both parents frequently posture in an upright warning stance as their young feed beside them. One adult regularly keeps watch while the other feeds.

Of course, the very nature of the young often gets them into trouble. When young birds stray too close to other feeding geese and fail to react to the threat postures correctly, their parents have to come to the rescue. The other goslings of course feel that they have to be involved and suddenly the whole family is adopting threat postures. Sometimes two or even three families meet in such a manner, which makes for highly entertaining but somewhat confusing watching.

Families of Brent and Whitefronts (opposite). The family bond is very strong and they move as a tight unit, any other members of the flock approaching too near to them are rapidly dealt with.

Returning individuals and site fidelity

Some individual geese have permanent distinctive markings that render them recognisable over long periods. These may be in the form of natural plumage variations or artificial markings such as coloured leg-rings or neck-collars inscribed with letters or numbers placed on the geese by man. These rings and collars are used to help unravel details of their movements and behaviour from their breeding grounds to wintering grounds to understand relationships between geese and to determine longevity. It is great to get to know individual geese by such markings, in particular natural variants, which are recognised by their appearance rather than an identification number. Their progress during the winter shows how the flocks move within the area and, in Pinkfeet, the interchanging of roost sites. Then, there is the pleasure of repeated sightings the following winter and the chance to see if they have a mate or goslings. Piecing together such sightings over several years has produced some interesting facts.

Pinkfeet, of which large numbers have been marked with rings and collars, have revealed detailed patterns of their movements within north Norfolk, to east Norfolk, to and from Lancashire, then to Scotland, on to the breeding grounds in Iceland, back again and so on.

Brent Geese have shown similar long journeys between their breeding grounds in northern Siberia, through locations such as the Netherlands to north Norfolk. Recognisable individual Brent Geese, and undoubtedly flocks, have exhibited remarkable site fidelity and have returned to the same locations for around twenty years. Whitefronts, on the other hand, remain more of a mystery.

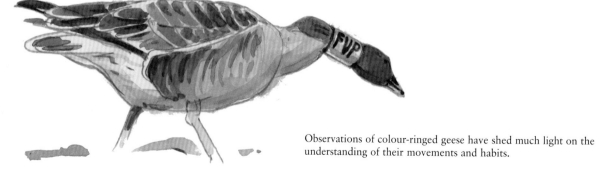

Observations of colour-ringed geese have shed much light on the understanding of their movements and habits.

Exercise and Feather Care

Plumage care, regular limbering up and stretching of limbs and bodies are essential duties that can be observed at regular intervals throughout the day. These ensure that birds are in good order for quick take-off without unnecessary strain and are in good shape for prolonged flight, if need be.

Preening and oiling

Preening is the most well-known of the essential activities of feather care. This process helps to keep the feathers in good condition, aiding insulation and efficient flight. Geese preening is a lovely activity to watch, as they gently work their bills through individual feathers from their quills outwards. Frequently they will break away from a particular tract of feathers, moving their attention to the base of the tail.

They have an oil gland there and a small amount of oil is released onto the bill then lightly smeared over the freshly manicured feathers. Any areas out of comfortable reach of the bill are oiled using the back of the head. It always looks a really enjoyable and satisfying process, heads thrown back, massaging the feathers of their upper backs and shoulders with the backs of their heads. Scratching is very much a part of preening and serves to clean the bill and clean and groom the feathers of the head and neck. When scratching delicate areas of the face the eye appears pale whitish; this is either the closed eye or the third eyelid, the nictating membrane, which comes across to help protect the eye.

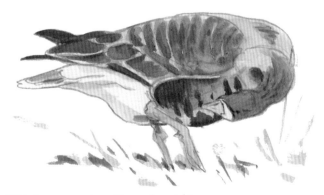

Whitefronts preening, oiling and scratching.

Brent Geese preening and drinking at low tide.

Feather care is essential for efficient flight and insulation against the elements. To reach every area and tract of feathers birds have to manoeuvre their bodies into extreme positions. These preening Brents produce some lovely shapes. One bird had a feather stuck to its bill following a lengthy bout of preening and had to shake its head violently in order to free it.

Pinkfeet preening. The sight of these large, bulky birds delicately manicuring their plumage is a beautiful action to watch.

Washing

Washing is another essential part of the maintenance routine and helps to remove from the plumage any dirt accumulated from daily living. Unlike preening, which can take place anywhere during the day, washing, by its nature, is more restricted. It may take place on the roost, or occasionally in a waterlogged dip of a feeding field. More often than not, however, it takes place at a favourite location such as fresh water flashes on the grazing meadows or, for Brents, in the mouths of fresh water sluices and shallow pools in the sand during low tide.

The larger grey geese are difficult to observe bathing but the lovely dark-coloured Brents are quite tame and easy to watch. Favourite locations such as Wells channel are perfect places to observe them and can lead to highly entertaining and rewarding goose-watching. After gathering on the sand, small groups walk or swim into the water and, after a few short bouts of preening, begin to wash.

Brent Geese and Black-headed Gulls gather together at pools and shallow water to wash - 6 February 2001.

Brents washing. This highly entertaining
behaviour is relatively easy to watch in harbour
channels and large creeks at low tide.

After surfacing many Brents have a habit of bill flexing, a stretch exercise that is also observed during preening.

Following energetic washing Brents will stand with their whole neck and body almost vertical and vigorously flap themselves dry, an action which resembles something between standing on tip-toes and hovering. Long bouts of preening and oiling follow, either in the water or on the sand. Washing is also a convenient time for a drink, although geese usually have other opportunities to drink while feeding. There are often small puddles in the fields or between furrows and, for Brents, a pool or creek nearby.

Following vigorous washing Brents stand bolt upright and flap themselves dry. An action that appears somewhere between standing on tip-toes and hovering.

Pair of Brents drinking.

Stretching and limbering up

Apart from external maintenance, physical exercises are equally important. They serve to keep the body, in particular the flight muscles and tendons, in good working order. Danger resulting in a sudden unexpected take-off puts considerable physical stress on the flight mechanisms and any injury could prove disastrous or even fatal.

A flightless or injured bird quickly becomes separated from the flock and is vulnerable to attacks by predators. So, constant limbering up can be observed at intervals throughout the day; before leaving the roost, during feeding and particularly during bouts of intensive preening and washing. If a flock feels wary or something has unsettled it, bouts of stretching run through the flock like wild-fire, for the geese know that they may be airborne in a split second.

16.01.00

The wing and leg stretch

In this exercise the wing, corresponding leg and tail-half are all stretched together. Firstly, the wing is stretched fully outwards along the length of the body, the leg is also stretched out and backwards and the tail-half fully fanned. The wing is then brought forward half-folded, while the leg and tail are relaxed before the wing is returned tightly folded against the body. It is a beautiful motion to watch, not only for the stretch and balance but also for the way the folded wing, with the exception of the very tips is 'swallowed' into a snug, perfectly fitting pocket made by the flank and shoulder (scapular) feathers. This stretch may be repeated on the opposite wing, leg and tail-half or frequently interspersed with another stretching routine which is described overleaf.

The simultaneous stretching of wing, tail and legs is an action of great balance and beauty.

In this next exercise both wings are stretched upwards and the 'hand', which holds the long primaries or wing-tips is kept folded. The head and neck remain upright or occasionally stretched slightly forward.

After stretching they often finish with, or at least include the following wing flutter. Both wings are flapped briefly but vigorously, then held spread out, slightly folded for a few moments before closing them.

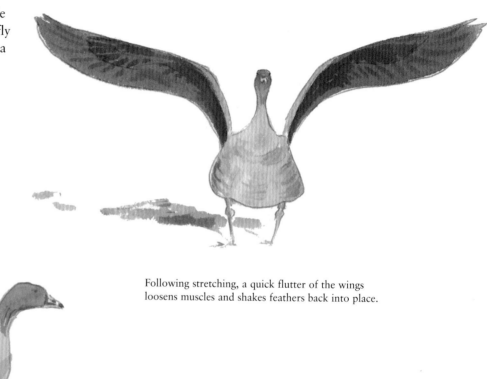

Following stretching, a quick flutter of the wings loosens muscles and shakes feathers back into place.

Both wings are stretched up together, each 'hand', holding the primary feathers or wingtips, is kept closed.

Take-off

The geese are relaxed and feeding, then suddenly the whole flock is airborne. The cause has been seen by at least one of the thousands of watchful pairs of eyes long before the observer notices. The take-off is followed by a crescendo of thousands of wingbeats and calls as the whole flock lifts. Despite appearing chaotic to us, order quickly begins to develop. Pairs, which have been separated, call to each other amongst the thousands of other voices; they recognize their mate returning their call and are soon reunited. The same is true of lost family members. Within a short while everyone knows where everyone is and the flock formations begin to take shape.

A sudden take-off sees the whole flock explode into the air - 9 December 2000.

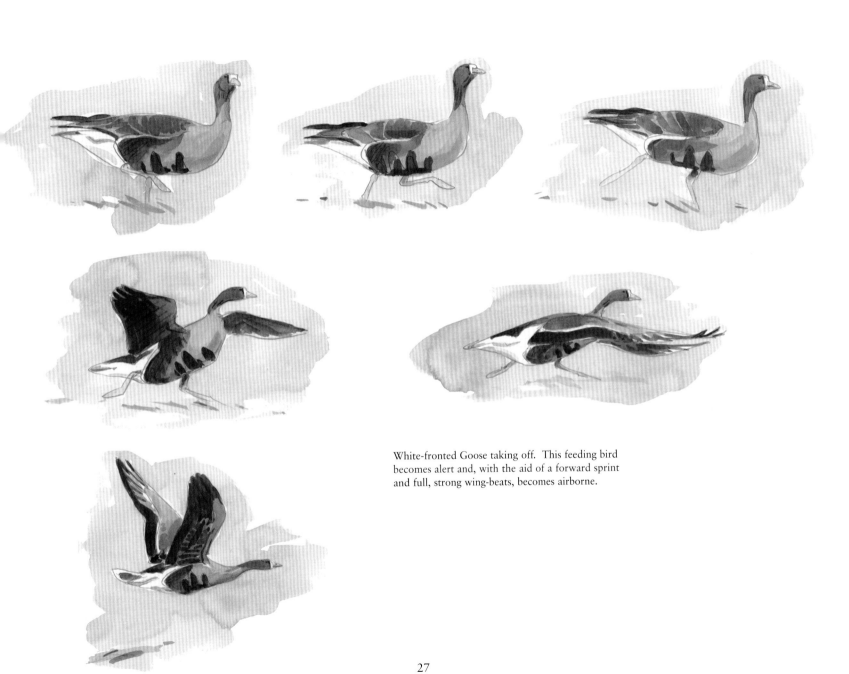

White-fronted Goose taking off. This feeding bird becomes alert and, with the aid of a forward sprint and full, strong wing-beats, becomes airborne.

Few would ever believe that the seemingly unruly bundle of Brents, whose flock is ever changing shape, contained any order at all. However, after a good bit of time, as it does take some believing, ordered groups of pairs and families join up within the bundle in small 'Vs', lines and arcs.

No one could argue that the vast lines and 'V' formations of Pinkfeet are not without order. A dominant bird, maybe one of the dominant ganders, takes the lead with its mate and, if they have any, their young follow behind in the slip stream. Sometimes it is possible to see well over a hundred birds in a single line alone. Pairs and families keep in touch by frequent calls, making sure that everyone is keeping up. Sometimes, between the large formations, a few families decide to remain in a separate family unit. This gives us a good opportunity to observe a startling range in the size of individuals, from the heavy-necked, thickset gander, through to the much smaller thin-necked juvenile goose. You would be forgiven for thinking, on first seeing this surprising size range, that you were looking at two separate species.

As the skeins reach their desired height, their flight path levels out and the flight action becomes much less laboured. On arrival at a new area flocks, on seeing other geese of their own kind, will simply glide down and drop in alongside them. If there are no geese present, flocks may circle nervously over the field many times before the first individuals summon up the courage to land. When the first geese have settled and look comfortable the rest of the flock will soon join them.

Brents are an exception. Not being a quarry species, they show much less caution and pitch down regardless at their leisure. They do, however, show greater caution around winter cereal crops from which they are actively discouraged.

Pinkfeet and Brent heading out to roost at Wells. The Pinkfeet arrive in vast lines and 'V' formations, whereas the Brent form an unruly bundle. Such flights are very noisy and are a good introduction to learning each species distinctive call. The ever evolving shape of Brent flocks sounding their lovely muttering calls and the sheer scale of the Pinkfeet skeins are among the high points of the winter landscape - January 2001.

Whiffling

Sometimes, if skeins are flying at a great height and want to lose altitude and momentum quickly, they employ a twisting, tumbling flight called whiffling. This spectacular feat can be truly breathtaking to watch, particularly when performed by a group of several thousand Pinkfeet. Initially, groups of geese cease flying and commence gliding, then suddenly, but quite literally, dive out of the sky with wings spread, the hand facing slightly back and necks stretched out. Then, while still diving, they proceed to turn upside down, right themselves, turn over the other way and so on, each goose taking its own path.

Contrary to some claims, they never perform a complete somersault. Occasionally a loud slap is heard as wing tips have collided. What makes this spectacle even more exciting is that during these aerobatics their heads are kept on the same plane. This detail is really worth looking out for if you are lucky enough to be in range to see it clearly.

When the geese feel they have lost sufficient height and speed they bank round and glide in to land while, high above them, other geese are beginning their own dives. This pattern continues until all the geese have landed. The overall effect of the flock could be likened to travelling down a river, over a waterfall and into turbulent rapids.

Pinkfeet whiffling. Gliding birds suddenly fall out of the sky in erratic dives, twists and turns in an attempt to lose height and momentum quickly. Occasionally the slap of two birds' wing feathers colliding can be heard - January 2001.

Landing

After gliding in, the geese will bank around to face the wind and then perform a series of rapid full wing beats to brake before they lightly touch down.

Pinkfeet and Brent Geese (right) coming into land. These Pinkfeet are gliding into a strong wind before landing - 7 January 2001.

Back to the roost

As dusk approaches the flock must soon make a decision as to when to head out to roost. I have sat watching Pinkfeet and Whitefronts well into dusk on several occasions in order to note their behaviour and to see if anything in particular prompts their departure. On every occasion, unless they were disturbed into flight, both species behaved in the same way. In the twilight the geese remained grazing but, as the dusk came and it began to grow darker, many geese ceased feeding and stood alert, their necks stretched vertically.

This stance was very similar to that of geese which have suddenly been disturbed and are ready to take flight but looked strange and unfamiliar since many birds around them were totally relaxed and still feeding. Gradually the majority of geese had become alert and had adopted the same stance. There was complete silence followed by a loud whoosh of wings, quickly followed by a chorus of excited calls; the whole flock was airborne and off to the roost. It is interesting to note that this was completely visual behaviour particularly bearing in mind that the light was often very poor and fading quickly. No calling prompted take-off.

Pinkfeet over Brancaster Quay on their way to their night-time roost on Scolt Head Island - 25 January 2000.

Pinkfeet flighting at dusk - January 2001.

Pink-footed Goose *Anser brachyrhynchus*

The Pink-footed Goose is one of the most familiar sights and sounds of the north Norfolk winter. Their large numbers can be a dominant feature of the winter landscape and their presence gives dynamic life and movement to the vast undulating farmland and open skies.

The Pinkfeet wintering in north Norfolk originate from Iceland and Greenland. This population, the majority of which nests in Iceland, is currently estimated at 225,000 birds, all of which winter in Scotland and northern and eastern England. A much smaller population of around 34,000 birds breeds in Svalbard and spends the winter in Denmark, Germany, the Netherlands and Belgium. In the last few years, the peak winter count in north Norfolk was estimated at over 76,000, representing over a third of the total Icelandic and Greenland population and over a quarter of the entire world population. It is exhilarating to realise that, after seeing a typical midwinter flight to or from a north Norfolk roost, you may have just seen over a tenth of the world's Pinkfeet within a few minutes.

The delicate shades of cold and warm greys and browns of the adult Pinkfeet changes continually with the light and viewing angle - 4 February 2000.

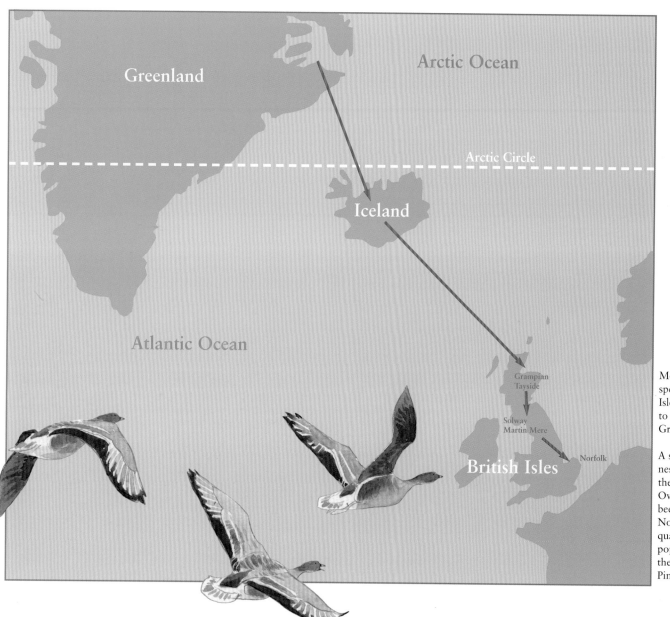

Greenland

Arctic Ocean

Arctic Circle

Iceland

Atlantic Ocean

Grampian
Tayside

Solway
Martin Mere

British Isles

Norfolk

Most of the world's Pinkfeet spend the winter in the British Isles and nest in Iceland and, to a lesser extent, in Greenland.

A smaller, separate population nests in Svalbard and spends the winter on the Continent. Over 76,000 Pinkfeet have been recorded in north Norfolk, representing over a quarter of the world population and over a third of the Icelandic and Greenland Pinkfeet.

Over a small space of sky above a Wells-next-the-Sea garden it has been possible to see over a sixth of the world population of Pinkfeet pass in the space of a few minutes. Jolly Sailor Yard - 31 December 2000.

The Pink-footed Goose was first described as a species in 1833. The first local and county record followed shortly afterwards in 1841 when a bird was shot at Holkham. This individual has been preserved and is still to be found in the 'Holkham Collection' at Holkham Hall.

The current winter population estimates are made from monthly co-ordinated dawn counts of geese, leaving the three traditional roosts, by a team of experienced counters. These roosts are to be found at the following coastal locations: in the Holkham and Wells area on intertidal sands east of Wells harbour, through Warham sandflats to Stiffkey; in the Brancaster area on the western tip of Scolt Head Island; finally on the mud and sand flats at the eastern side of The Wash at Snettisham.

The pattern of use of these roosting areas has changed over time so each is treated separately.

Comparisons are then made of combined wintering populations, starting with the first co-ordinated counts and continuing to those of the present day.

Evening flight over Wells-next-the-Sea - January 2001.

Holkham and Wells

After the original record in 1841, many others were identified at Holkham where they were regarded as the commonest species of goose. During this period Pinkfeet appeared to feed predominantly on the fresh marshes at Holkham and roosted between Wells harbour and Stiffkey. This pattern continued into the next century, with numbers reaching a peak in the 1930s when around 8000 were recorded. During this time they were beginning to be noted flighting inland to feed on fields of stubble and ley grass. This period was glorified by early books and paintings about shorebirds and wildfowling by Frank Southgate and Peter Scott, in the writings of W.H.Hudson and documented in the diaries of Pat Crinkle.

In 1938 everything suddenly changed. The salt marshes and sands off Warham and Stiffkey became an anti-aircraft firing range and during the war years that were to follow the grazing marshes at Holkham came under the plough. Needless to say, the Pinkfeet deserted and it was not until 1963 that a group of 50 were seen at Wells. Pinkfeet, however, remained rare in the area until the early 1980s with isolated peak counts of 100 in 1974 and 250 in 1976. Nevertheless, the excitement felt by at least one local who had known them in his youth before the onset of war was evident in his announcement, 'the Pinks are back, the Pinks are back'.

In the winter of 1982-83 a group of 300 settled for part of the winter at Holkham and since then the Pinkfeet have returned each year. Their numbers have steadily increased with counts of around 50,000 recorded at the end of December 2000.

The Scolt Head Island Roost

The history of this roost, which is located at the western end of Scolt Head Island, is comparatively recent. The first ever record of Pinkfeet using it was on the 20th November 1979 when 90 geese roosted and continued to use it until the 19th January 1980. Since then numbers have continually strengthened and reached a peak of 52,000 in January 2001. Although a surprisingly recent development, the term 'traditional roost' is accepted locally.

Snettisham Roost

This roost, on the mudflats of the Wash, should strictly speaking, be regarded as north-west Norfolk. There is, however, so much interchange between the three roosts and daily feeding areas that it is very much a feature of the lives of Pinkfeet in north Norfolk. Pinkfeet have been recorded in this area since the early 1900s, although the actual records are quite fragmented. In January 1956, 329 Pinkfeet were counted and it is believed that around two or three hundred could be found in the area during most winters until the late 1960s. In 1968 accurate counts commenced and a peak count of 843 was made in February of that year. Since then numbers have steadily risen and a peak count of 45,925 was recorded in January 1994.

1985-86	19,900	1990-91	42,950	1995-96	54,760
1986-87	19,800	1991-92	35,060	1996-97	55,500
1987-88	18,800	1992-93	33,880	1997-98	76,170
1988-89	13,500	1993-94	68,560	1998-99	76,355
1989-90	26,920	1994-95	53,540	1999-2000	64,770

Combined peak totals from the co-ordinated counts illustrate the steady increase in the north Norfolk population.

Pinkfeet have been remarkably consistent in their arrival dates. In recent years the first birds have arrived right at the end of the second week of September, the earliest date being the 10th September. The newly arrived flocks, which often number between a dozen and thirty, spend most of their time feeding on the grazing marshes or nearby stubble and remain to roost on the grazing marshes during the first few weeks of their stay. During this period the numbers soon build up to several hundred birds. By October numbers are generally into four figures and sometime during the first half of the month the flocks begin to flight across to the traditional roost site on the sands. It is probably no coincidence that around this time skeins also begin to venture into the farmland that borders the coast, just as the sugar-beet harvest gets underway. Sugar-beet is the favoured food of Pinkfeet in this area. The geese feed on the tops which have been mechanically chopped off and discarded after the root has been gathered up by the tractor-pulled harvesters. This food preference has been noted in the area since the mid to late 1960s.

Pinkfeet sorting through sugar-beet tops left behind after the roots have been harvested.

The numbers at all three sites build up more rapidly towards the end of October and by the middle of November the bulk of the winter population should have arrived and can be seen flighting each morning out to the freshly-harvested beet fields. Pinkfeet are surprisingly fickle about their choice of feeding places, having favoured areas throughout the region.

The reason for this is probably to do with the aspect of the land, the flock requiring good vantage points and safe flight paths to and from the fields. This fussiness is evident when large numbers continue to feed on a field which has been reduced to near-bare earth when, only a few fields away is a newly-harvested one, full of tops which they will never visit.

The flock will work its way through the patchwork of harvested fields until the supply of tops becomes exhausted or is ploughed in.

This fact begins to emerge in mid-February when flocks of Pinkfeet begin to frequent the grazing marshes once more. Usually, prior to this movement to grass, a drop in numbers is frequently noticed in late January. This is due to the fact that some groups have moved north to the next staging post in Lancashire.

By March numbers are falling continually and most remaining birds can be seen for long periods on the grazing marshes. By the end of March the bulk has departed and only small numbers linger for a short while, although occasionally a handful will stay on as late as May. Currently there are far more Pinkfeet in north Norfolk than have ever been documented. Due to our knowledge of the past climate and vegetation it wouldn't be too speculative to suggest that there are more wintering in north Norfolk than there have ever been. This is certainly a comforting thought.

Adult and young pinkfeet. Young birds appear quite tatty and mottled as their juvenile feathers are gradually replaced by new adult-like ones. The unusually marked bird (top) has a white breast and wing-tips. This is a recurring pattern and is sometimes referred to as schizochromic. Such individuals are encountered in most winters. More rarely all white, frosty-grey and biscuit-coloured birds have also been seen.

Pinkfeet gliding and whiffling in to land over oaks. The rounded, wind-sculptured canopy and zig-zag branches of the oaks are a familiar sight of the open farmland. Their silhouettes along with Pinkfeet and Woodpigeons are typical components of the winter landscape of inland farmland - 24 January 2000.

In the tight, densely-packed flocks lots of antagonistic behaviour is often seen. Other birds, such as as these Pied Wagtails, are attracted to the newly-harvested fields and it is not unusual to see small flocks feeding around the Pinkfeet - January 2000.

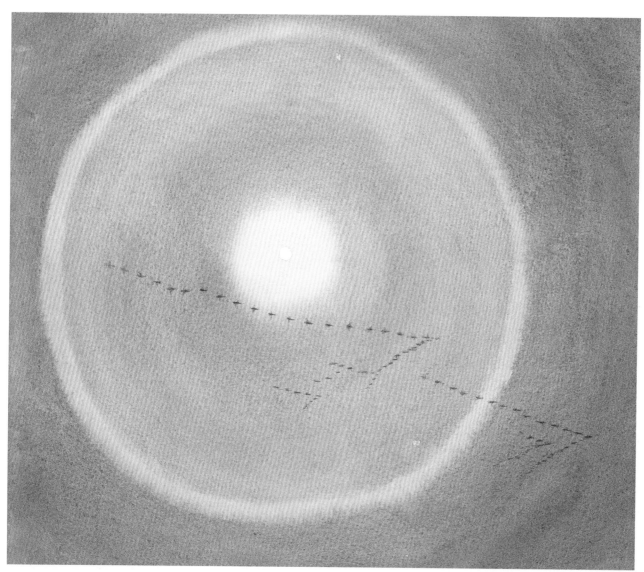

Pinkfeet in front of a hazy moon and its halo as they head inland to feed in the moonlight - 31 December 1998.

New arrivals join the flock - 1 December 2000.

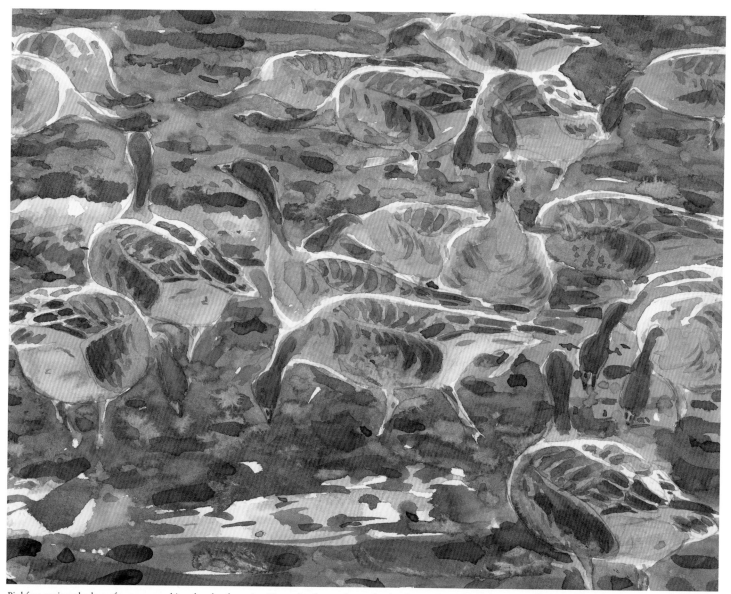

Pinkfeet against the low afternoon sunshine shortly after rain. Two pairs threatening each other break the calm and add some drama to the peaceful scene - February 2000.

Coastal fog. On this particular day, as sunshine broke through patches in the fog, warm coloured feathers on the sides of the Pinkfeet's necks were strongly highlighted and shone copper - 3 February 2001.

Pinkfeet in a snow blizzard - 29 December 2000.

By midday the sun had begun to break through and by late afternoon much of the snow had melted - 29 December 2000

Pinkfeet commuting between feeding areas, just before rain, Wighton Village - 29 November 2000

Pinkfeet feeding on sugar-beet tops against the low, soft winter sunlight - 6 January 2001.

To lose height rapidly the flock begins to whiffle; amazingly during these erractic twists and tumbles their heads are kept on the same plane - 4 December 2000.

Soon after dawn the first Pinkfeet arrive on the sugar-beet tops. In the low farmland behind, mist begins to rise and promises a fine morning - 7 January 2000.

As dusk approaches seemingly endless skeins of Pinkfeet pass over Wells harbour towards their roost site on the vast tidal sands - December 1999.

White-fronted Geese at Holkham. The closer pair have their three goslings feeding close beside them - February 2000.

White-fronted Goose *Anser albifrons*

White-fronted Geese have only one regular wintering site in the region, the grazing marshes at Holkham where they are regarded as a speciality. The Whitefronts at Holkham belong to the nominate race *Anser a. albifrons*, which breed on the tundra regions of northern Russia and Siberia. Many birds wintering in the Netherlands, Belgium, England and Wales are known, through ringing recoveries, to breed in northern Arkhangelsk on the White Sea coast, the Kanin Peninsula, the island of Kolguev and Novaya Zemlya, with a few recoveries east to the Taymyr Peninsular. It is most likely that the Holkham birds breed somewhere within these areas.

Arctic Ocean

Novaya Zemlya

Taymyr

Arctic Circle

Kanin Kolguev

Arkhangelsk

Moscow

British Isles

At Holkham one of the first recorded sightings was of 20 birds in December 1851. It would appear that a similar pattern of occurrence continued until at least 1890. There is very little information about their status until the mid-1930s when over 250 were recorded. There is, again, very little further information from the war years. This is unfortunate, as it would have been interesting to see how they fared at a time when large areas of the grazing marshes were under the plough. It is unlikely that they totally abandoned the area, as similar numbers were regularly present during the winters immediately after the war.

Then, for unknown reasons, in 1951 their numbers declined to around 100 birds. The following winters saw a further decline with irregular records of up to 50 birds. In the winter of 1968-69, the number rose to 84 and since then, with the exception of a couple of poor years, their numbers have slowly risen and begun to stabilise with usually around 260-300 birds present most winters. These numbers are regularly boosted by small influxes in February and again in March. Such an influx in March 1996 resulted in a record peak of over 800 Whitefronts.

The Whitefronts are the latest arrivals of our regular wintering geese. Birds have been seen in the first week of October but it is usually in the second week that the first birds arrive. The main numbers, however, do not arrive until after Christmas.

Young birds in the early winter lack their parents black belly-bars and white forehead. However, as the season progresses, the young begin to moult and their white foreheads and first black belly feathers start to show.

In past years Whitefronts roosted either on the same tidal sands, between Wells Harbour and Stiffkey, that the Pinkfeet use as their roost, or occasionally on the open sea. During the 1980s they were often noted staying on the grazing marshes to roost as well as on the sandflats. As the water levels at Holkham grazing marshes have become better managed and the water drainage system greatly improved, the water levels are now much higher, enabling the Whitefronts to choose to roost on large open flashes between Lady Anne's Drive and Meols House. During some of the larger influx years the newly-arrived birds, despite feeding with the regular winter flock, have formed their own separate flock at dusk and flighted out to the sands with the Pinkfeet, flighting back at dawn each morning to rejoin the other Whitefronts to feed.

During the 1970s and up until the early 1990s, the Whitefronts' preferred feeding area was the fields at the Burnham Overy end of the grazing marshes. Here they were almost always very distant, shy and difficult to observe properly. Changes to the management of these fields, in the form of more intensive mowing and grazing, made them less suitable for Whitefronts, who prefer rougher, drier, less intensively managed fields. Suddenly, much to everyone's surprise, they began to use the fields each side of Lady Anne's Drive, the popular and frequently busy road leading to Holkham beach. This has now become their regular feeding area and the flock has become surprisingly tolerant of the large number of people and cars. This situation now provides probably the best views of wild Russian White-fronted Geese anywhere in the country.

Two families of White-fronted Geese feeding amongst the mole-hills on the grazing marshes. One of the adults from the left hand family chases away a youngster from the other family and is, in turn, met with a threat from one of its parents - February 2000.

Variations in the belly-bars of White-fronted Geese at Holkham. Surprisingly, studies have shown that these markings on individual birds vary from year to year.

Two White-fronted Goose families - 6 February 2000.

Whitefronts flapping over a fence to reach another feeding area. Frequent watching is the best way to become familiar with the appearance, habits and high-pitched yapping calls of this beautiful goose - 20 February 2001.

Holkham is the only traditional wintering site for Whitefronts in the region.
Here they prefer the drier, rough grazing fields - February 2000.

The first Brent Geese of the season. These newly-arrived birds make a beeline for the pockets of Eel-grass along the coast - 21 September 1998.

Dark-bellied Brent Goose *Branta b.bernicla*

The soft muttering calls and characteristically untidy flocks of this attractive, small, dark goose are very evocative of winter days on the north Norfolk coast. Locally they are simply referred to as Brents or Brants. Brent Goose is, in fact, a corruption of Brant Goose, whose origins have been traced back to the Old Norse –Brandgás which simply means burnt goose, where burnt is understood to mean black.

Our winter flocks of Brents belong to the dark-bellied nominate race *B.b.bernicla*. This race breeds on the riversides, coasts and off-shore islands and islets of northern Russia and Siberia, from the island of Kolguev, eastwards to just beyond the Taymyr Peninsula. The coastline around the Taymyr holds the largest numbers. The entire population of this race winters in the Netherlands, western France and southern and eastern England, with large numbers spending either side of mid-winter in Denmark and West Germany.

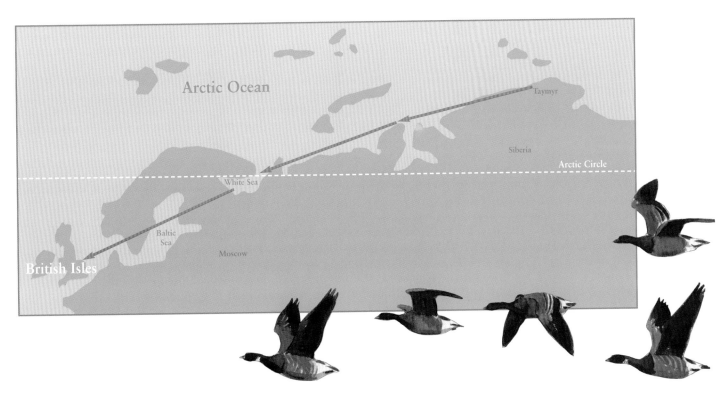

A family of Brents migrating together.

The early history of the Brents in north Norfolk is poorly documented. In the records for the late 1800s they were regarded as a common winter visitor, with the only indication of the size of the winter population coming from Blakeney Harbour where it ranged between one and three hundred. During these times, Brents were an entirely maritime species and were seldom seen away from salt water. In the early 1900s Brents were still regarded as common and, although no counts were recorded, it is likely that similar numbers were present.

The 1930s marked the beginning of a disastrous period for the Dark-bellied Brent Goose when the world population rapidly crashed. At the same time one of the Brents' favourite and most important foods, the Common Eel-grass *Zostera marina,* was wiped out from huge areas of coastal north-west Europe. This plant was known locally as Wigeon grass and, prior to the disease, existed in extensive thick beds way below the tideline of sheltered harbours and estuaries such as those at Wells and Blakeney.

Initially it was believed that the drastic disappearance of this species of Eel-grass was the main cause of the rapid fall in the Brent population. It later transpired that other factors were also major contributors. Over-exploitation of the birds in the form of shooting and the collecting of eggs, combined with consecutive poor breeding seasons, all played major roles. Another possible contributing factor has recently come to light. It is suggested that large numbers of Brents' eggs, goslings and moulting adults, which are temporarily flightless, were collected annually to help feed the inmates of Stalin's Siberian gulag camps.

Thankfully the species was awarded full protection throughout its range and the population slowly but steadily began to recover. It was not until the mid-1970s, however, that the population reached its pre-1930 levels. From that time the numbers have increased and the breeding range has even begun to spread to new areas to the east of the Taymyr Peninsula.

In the mid 1950s, the entire world population of Dark-bellied Brents was only 16,500 birds. In 1960 the number had risen to 22,000 and by 1970 had reached 39,000. By 1973, following two very good breeding seasons, the number had risen to 80,000 birds. During this period a new change in feeding habits from marine plants to grass and cereal crops aided their recovery and further expansion, although this habit was not recorded in north Norfolk until the 1980s. The current world population is estimated at somewhere between 250,000 and 300,000.

This recovery and subsequent expansion in numbers is directly mirrored in the records of winter flocks in north Norfolk. In 1953, the highest flock recorded was one of only 150-200 birds at Blakeney. By 1963 counts at Blakeney had reached 2500-3000, with further flocks of 500 at Brancaster and 1500 at Wells. By 1994 the wintering population in north Norfolk was almost 15,000 birds, only 1500 less than the entire world population in 1955. Co-ordinated counts between Holme and Salthouse in February 1996 produced a maximum of 14,803 and another count in 1997 produced an estimate of 14,088.

Brents suddenly become alert and vocal before deciding to fly into Wells Harbour to wash and preen during low tide. The wide variation in the size and shape of the neck markings is obvious in these alert birds.

64

21 Nov 00   Wells Quay   Flowing tide

Three pairs loafing around the last remaining areas of sand as the flowing tide quickly fills Wells Channel - 21 November 2000.

Breeding success varies dramatically and can be easily seen by the percentage of young birds present within the flock. In good years there may be as many as 50% young, while in poor years there may be none at all. Successful breeding attempts can result in pairs with up to six goslings. Observations from the wintering grounds have shown that there was a peak in the number of juveniles roughly every three years. Furthermore, this seemed to coincide with peaks in numbers of young wading birds such as Knot, Sanderling and Turnstone, which had breeding populations nesting in the same area as the Brents.

On-going work that has been taking place over the last decade by a team of Dutch and Russian scientists and field observers has helped clarify this situation; it has also uncovered some fascinating facts and insights into the lives of the Dark-bellied Brents. Work on the Taymyr Peninsula has shed light on these three-year peaks and has found that these correspond to similar peaks in the life cycle of lemmings and their predators. Some of the main findings are summarised here. Their detailed findings make fascinating reading and are worth following up in greater detail.

On the Russian tundra there is a peak in the populations of lemmings on average every three years. In the following season their numbers crash and lemmings are very scarce. This fluctuation greatly affects the numbers, habits and breeding success of predators, notably Arctic Foxes and Snowy Owls which feed on them. Only in good lemming years are they able to bring up large numbers of young.

Young Brents are distinguished from their parents by fine white tips to their covert feathers, which form neat white lines on their backs.

Consequently, in the following year the number of predators will be high but the number of lemmings very low.

Snowy Owls, by their nature, are nomadic wanderers of Arctic regions, many often moving with the food supply; some, however, stay. Arctic Foxes on the other hand will remain; both predators now have to turn their attention to other food sources. In such years the bird populations which migrate to these remote regions to breed will be greatly affected by these predators and very few young will fledge. This natural cycle explains the average of three-year peaks in high numbers of young Brents and wading birds.

Interestingly, Brents will nest on the mainland during peak Lemming years, since the predators show little interest in them. Several pairs will also, in such years, choose to nest within close proximity to Snowy Owls' nests, as the owls give them extra protection due to the simple fact that they will not tolerate Arctic Foxes or other predators anywhere near their own nests.

Back in north Norfolk the first Brents to arrive back are seen during the third week of September, usually between the 15th and 19th, with most of the birds arriving in October and early November. During this period good numbers can be seen arriving or moving west along the coastline, especially during periods of strong on-shore winds and poor visibility, when parties pass close in-shore, frequently along the breakers.

In years with good breeding success the first family parties are normally encountered by mid-October, occasionally as early as late September. By December the bulk of the birds will have arrived and settled into their mid-winter routines. Mid to late March sees the majority of Brents departing, although some flocks of up to several hundred birds may remain to feed on the salt marshes as late as early May. The vast majority of these are paired up and rather than being non-breeding birds, as has been suggested, it is quite likely that they choose to feed here rather than join the large concentrations at migration posts in the Netherlands, Denmark and West Germany. Bearing in mind that the first Brents do not reach the breeding grounds in the Taymyr until mid-June, they still have plenty of time to get there.

Northerly gales force migrating Brents, and pelagic birds like these storm-blown Little Auks, close in shore. Cley beach - 10 November 1999.

New arrivals and feeding habits

The first arrivals back always make a bee-line for the handful of small pockets of Eel-grass dotted along the coast. On the favoured arrival dates it is always exciting to look across these areas, such as the low mudflats to the east of Wells Harbour mouth, to see if any Brents have arrived to join the first few Wigeon feeding there. From the lifeboat-house they may only appear as grey, black and white goose-shaped specks but they are undeniably Brents. For those who are interested and have a feel for the north Norfolk coast, its seasons and wildlife, the satisfaction of seeing the first returning geese is akin to the sight of the first swallow of spring.

These surviving Eel-grass beds are made up of two species, the most common being the Dwarf Eel-grass *Zostera noltii*, which forms short lawns of straight, thin leaves. Mixed in are small isolated patches of the slightly larger Narrow-leaved Eel-grass *Zostera angustifolia*. These two small species did not appear to suffer from the same disease that killed off the extensive beds of their larger cousin.

As September progresses the daily feeding and increasing numbers of both Brents and Wigeon soon exhaust these areas and green lines of washed-up leaves on the neighbouring shores become a brief localised landmark of late September. The geese move on to other favoured foods in the harbours such as the green algae *Enteromorpha* and, on higher areas and salt marshes, they are frequently seen feeding on Samphire *Salicornia* beds and on grasses such as the Saltmarsh Grass *Puccinellia maritima*.

At the beginning of the 20th century flocks would have remained feeding on such areas and plants throughout their stay. As the Brents' population began to recover, flocks began to feed on neighbouring grassland. This was soon followed by grazing on winter cereal, which made them unpopular with the farming community and in the 1970s flocks were beginning to venture much further inland.

They are now a regular sight, particularly in mid-winter on grazing marshes and farmland, as well as showing preferences for short mown grassy areas such as the football pitch, the pitch and putt course and even in between areas of caravans along the Beach Road at Wells, a far cry from the Siberian tundra.

Flocks roosting at Warham have regularly travelled as far inland as Langham and Field Dalling. In late winter and early spring, larger numbers begin to feed on the higher salt marshes, seeking out new growth of species like Sea Aster *Aster tripolium* and the grass, *Puccinellia maritima*. The flocks spend their nights at several roosts situated in the main harbour channels or in the large undisturbed creeks along the length of the coast.

Small beds and pockets of Dwarf and Narrow-leaved Eel-grasses are the best places to look for the first returning Brents.

Newly-landed Brents have dropped in too closely to other pairs and families and are quickly moved on before order returns to the flock. The vibrations from the feet and bills of these densely-packed, fast-feeding Brents seem to have a similar effect on earthworms as rainfall does and causes them to rise to the surface. Ever the opportunist, Black-headed Gulls are quick to exploit this food and small numbers walk amongst, or fly above the Brents. The slower-moving and less densely packed flocks of grey geese often fail to have the same effect and frequently do not attract the gulls - 28 January 2000.

The sheltered harbours at low tide, particularly where fresh water sluices or springs are found, are great places to watch Brents washing. Here they are regularly joined by other species like these Black-headed Gulls. Their antics are both fascinating and entertaining to watch.

20.02.04 Wyns Harbour low water   brent + cold

Brent Geese feeding in the mist on the pitch and putt course on Wells Beach Road - 1 February 2001.

Early spring sees a change in the behaviour of the Brents. The pair bond becomes even more evident and elements of courtship are seen in the form of lengthy chases between three and, very rarely, four Brents. This involves a single goose being pursued by two or more ganders. It would appear that these chases involve either unpaired ganders pursuing an unpaired goose or an unpaired gander trying to split up a pair and win the favour of the goose. These lengthy chases usually end in a pair and the remaining gander landing in separate parts of the flock. More occasionally the three geese will split up and land in different areas of the flock.

These situations have appeared to end in passive agreements. Very rarely have chases ended in physical fights with the two ganders, locked together each gripping their opponent with their bill and trying to prevent a blow from the strong bony wing joint. The victorious gander wins the attention of the goose and walks towards her gesturing proudly. The goose and gander seem to have made progress in becoming a pair and walk back to the flock together. In the meantime the defeated gander has already returned submissively to another part of the flock. These observations help confirm the idea that pairs are formed in the winter quarters.

As the spring progresses many Brents will have moved on to other migration staging posts across the North Sea. The behaviour of the remaining Brents which linger into May changes still further. These flocks, which remain to feed exclusively on the salt marshes and shore, become increasingly more fragmented and the distances between individual pairs greater. Only their young, if they have any, will be permitted close to them. Frequent head flicking and dipping is regularly noted which show elements of premating rituals and that the Brents are coming into breeding condition.

This courtship behaviour is noted at the various stop-off locations; actual mating however, does not take place until they arrive on their nesting grounds. The flocks, however, do come together in certain situations such as high tide loafing, communal washing and at the night-time roost. In such situations there is usually lots of antagonism and threatening behaviour. These combined flocks now number only a hundred or so.

The longer daylight hours and warmer growing conditions allow the Brents to gain much weight, which is essential for their long migrations ahead. Several traditional stop-offs will be made to replenish their fat reserves en route to the breeding grounds. In common with all geese, this fat is stored between the belly and tail and, just prior to leaving, can sometimes be distinctly seen. It is especially important for the female, who will soon be producing eggs and incubating them for long periods in the cold Siberian tundra, while her mate guards the nesting territory. Studies have found that the heaviest geese have by far the best chances of producing young.

One morning in early or mid May it is apparent that the flocks have departed. Very occasionally you may be fortunate to see the final departure when the Brents come together once more as a tight flock and suddenly rise, calling continuously and head strongly northwards out to sea.

Actual fighting is very rare amongst geese. Here two ganders fight for the attention of the goose. Wells-next-the-Sea – March 2001.

High-speed chases involving two ganders and a goose begin to be a regular spectacle during the late winter and early spring. These lengthy chases usually end without incident but very occasionally, as we have seen, they can end in the two ganders fighting, the victor appearing to gain the attention of the goose.

Recognisable individuals and abberant birds

As one would expect, the occurrence of atypically-coloured or unusually marked individuals amid the thousands of wintering Brents is a regular phenomenon. One of the most common abnormalities is that of birds with mottled white heads. Usually this mottling begins as a continuation of the white neck markings and continues onto the back of the head and cheeks, becoming less dense towards the eye. These birds are otherwise typically marked. More rarely, sandy and grey-coloured birds have been seen.

One pale grey bird has returned to the area for over 18 years and has affectionately become known as the 'Silver Brent' by local goose enthusiasts who hope for and look forward to its arrival each winter. Its history of occurrence in the area is interesting and gives a perfect example of site fidelity in certain individual Brent Geese.

This leucistic bird has been a regular feature of the coastal marshes around Brancaster harbour since November 1982. It is an exceptionally beautiful individual and is especially attractive when seen flighting amongst a large flock of Brents, then dropping down to feed on the marshes on a crisp winter's day. Initially it appeared along with an identical sibling, flying west at Cley in October 1982. They were next noted in the Brancaster harbour area in

November of that year where they remained for the rest of the winter. The following year they appeared at Wells during the early winter period before moving on to Brancaster for the rest of the season.

In the following winter, 1984-85, only one bird returned but it has continued to return to the Brancaster harbour area ever since. When feeding or washing out in the harbour it can be difficult to observe; however, the adjacent marshes of Burnham Norton and Deepdale offer better opportunities to see it. It is clearly paired to a typically marked Brent but during its time here it has only been noted once with young, all of which were typically marked.

A sandy coloured Brent Goose -
30 November 1993, Wells Harbour

January 1999

The leucistic 'Silver Brent' which, seen amongst a flock of Brents, is a beautiful sight. This particular individual has graced the north Norfolk coast since October 1982.

As spring approaches the pair bond becomes tighter and the distances between pairs greater. The groups do, however, come together at certain times such as roosting, communal washing and when they are ready to migrate. Here a young Pale-bellied Brent which has spent the winter with the flock, becomes increasingly isolated - 14 April 2001.

Holkham 8·2·99

For those with keen eyes and a little patience, further interest is added to our winter Brent flocks by way of two other races of Brent Geese. These are the Pale-bellied Brent and the Black Brant, both of which are rare but regular visitors to the region - 8 February 1999.

Pale-bellied Brent *Branta bernicla hrota*

This attractive form differs from our Brent in having its flanks and belly chalky-white, sharply contrasting with its blackish neck, and in its back colour, which has a brownish tone. This race breeds in Svalbard, Arctic Canada and north-east Greenland. The Svalbard birds winter in Denmark and in northern England in Northumberland.

The majority of the Canadian Arctic birds winter on the Atlantic coast of the United States. The remaining birds from Canada, together with the Greenland population, winter in Ireland. In most years one or two birds will be seen within a couple of flocks of Brent along the coast here in Norfolk. Much rarer are small influxes and, very occasionally, singles which have been seen amongst the large inland-feeding Pinkfeet flocks. The small numbers mixed in with the Brents are most likely to have originated from the Svalbard population, having been caught up in the Dark-bellied Brent flocks in places such as Denmark, where their migration routes overlap. A few individuals seem to form some kind of bond with their new companions and must migrate to Siberia with them since they are seen with the same flocks, in the same location, for several consecutive winters.

This suspicion was strengthened by the reappearance of one such bird, recognisable by a distinctive limp, which returned to Wells for several winters. Despite these particular Pale-bellied Brents' strong associations with certain Dark-bellied flocks, none of these returning individuals has ever been noted paired-up. However, a Pale and a Dark-bellied Brent were seen acting as a pair and were in loose company with a pair of Dark-bellied Brents on a spring morning on Wells salt marsh.

Svalbard is most likely to be the origin of the occasional small flocks and influxes. Their arrival on this coast takes the form of small numbers at various locations or the sudden appearance of small flocks which have numbered as many as 38. Such flocks usually avoid the direct company of the larger Dark-bellied flocks or may associate loosely with them, preferring to stay in an isolated group. This behaviour, along with a noticeable tendency to be tamer was noted in the Blakeney area in the late 19th century and even led to them becoming known as 'Stranger Brents' in that vicinity.

A pair of Pale-bellied Brents seeing off a Dark-bellied Brent.

James McCallum.

This pair of Pale-bellied Brents was part of a small influx which associated
only loosely with the geese at Lady Anne's Drive, Holkham - 9 January 1998.

In the early months of 1996, an influx of Pale-bellied Brent was noted at many localities along the coast. Amongst a group of 17 birds at Holkham were two carrying colour rings. These rings confirmed that Svalbard was indeed the origin of these birds and also provided us with some insights into their movements.

They had originally been ringed in Lindisfarne, Northumberland, in December 1991 as part of a scientific study. The normal pattern of movements would be to spend the mid-winter in Northumberland, then migrate to Denmark where they could be found between February and May before moving on to Svalbard to nest. However, in 1996 they were seen in Northumberland on 24th January and were next seen at Holkham on 27th February, where they remained until 6th March.

They were next observed in Holland on 12th March and were back on familiar territory, in Denmark, on 4th April. They remained there until 11th May before continuing their journey to Svalbard. The 5th December that year saw them back in Northumberland.

The sightings of Pale-bellied Brents with Pinkfeet almost certainly involve birds from the Greenland and Arctic Canada population which would normally be spending the winter in Ireland. An important migration staging-post for Pale-bellied Brents bound for Ireland is Iceland. It is likely that it is here, or Greenland, that the odd one gets mixed up with the Pinkfeet and eventually ends up in north Norfolk. Interestingly, their Latin name, *hrota*, originates from the Icelandic for Brent Goose.

Pale-bellied Brents associating with the vast Pinkfeet flocks are most likely to be of Greenland origin - 2 January 2001.

Black Brant *Branta bernicla nigricans*

This striking form is recognised by its highly contrasting, almost black and white plumage. This, combined with a large broad neck collar that meets under the chin, renders it a very handsome goose.

Its back and belly are, in fact, sooty brown and show little contrast with the black neck but are clearly demarcated from the whitish half-moon flank patch.

A Black Brant swims amongst the other Brents constantly calling, presumably looking for a companion of its own kind - 2 March 2001.

The Black Brant breeds in northern Siberia, east from the Taymyr Peninsula, in Alaska and in Arctic Canada. It winters on both sides of the Pacific, principally on the eastern side. The Black Brant breeding in Siberia, wintering on the western coast of the Pacific and known as the Asia-Pacific population, has undergone a steady decline in numbers due to hunting pressures on its migration routes and wintering grounds. However, birds breeding in America and Canada and wintering on the eastern Pacific coasts have fared much better. They have rapidly expanded their breeding range westwards into Siberia and now nest as far west as the Taymyr Peninsula. In recent years the breeding areas of our Dark-bellied Brents and Black Brants have begun to overlap. These facts, combined with a greater awareness of the field appearance of the Black Brant, have resulted in a sudden increase in numbers and sightings of this goose in western Europe.

In north Norfolk the Black Brant was first recorded in 1982, when an adult was identified at Cley on the 7th November. Black Brants are exclusively seen within the large Brent flocks and many records refer to the same returning individuals. For example, the original Cley bird returned for six winters and was last seen on 12 March, 1989. It was not until 1988 that a fresh individual was seen. One or two birds wintering in the area became the regular pattern until the late 1990s when the records suddenly increased. In the winter months of 1998/99 at least six different birds were noted in north Norfolk. This sudden explosion in numbers locally was mirrored elsewhere in Britain and Europe. This change was undoubtedly caused by the expansion and overlapping of the breeding ranges of the two forms and the resulting higher chance of Black Brants becoming mixed in with our migrating Brents. A team of ornithologists visiting an area where breeding ranges overlapped found a small number of mixed pairs of Black Brants and Dark-bellied Brents. Evidence of successful mixed pairings has been noted on their wintering grounds in Europe on three occasions. The most recent of

these was in north Norfolk, when a Black Brant gander together with his Dark-bellied mate, arrived with four hybrid young at Burnham Deepdale in January 2001. It would seem that the evolution of Brent Goose forms is far from complete and if the Black Brant continues to expand its numbers and range westwards it will be interesting to observe what further changes may develop.

Interestingly the first recorded pair of pure Black Brants with young in western Europe has recently been seen in the Netherlands. How long will it be before a similar situation is witnessed on this coast? At present we can only speculate as to whether these are isolated cases or the beginnings of change. Whatever the future brings it certainly adds further excitement and interest to an already charismatic group.

A mixed pair of Black Brant and Dark-bellied Brent with their four hybrid young. These young shared many features closer to their father, the Black Brant. Their mother was distinctive in that she had a couple of white feathers in her right-hand wing coverts - 13 February 2001.

Regular Visitors

Although not traditional wintering species, Barnacle and Bean Geese are seen each year in small numbers

Barnacle Goose *Branta leucopsis*

The Barnacle Goose is fractionally larger than the Brent with noticeably longer wings, which give the body a longer appearance when at rest. The combination of cream or white faces contrasting with their short black necks carries well over long distances. These features, together with the blue-grey back which is marked with blackish bars, often with a white tip, and the lovely pale grey flanks, produce a unique appearance which is instantly recognisable. Young birds, although still highly distinctive, lack the crisp contrast of the adults; their necks have a greyer cast and their backs and flanks have a slightly 'moth-eaten' appearance due to the unmoulted juvenile feathers mixed in with new, crisp adult like feathers.

There are three traditional populations of Barnacle Geese. Birds breeding in east Greenland migrate via Iceland to winter in western Scotland and Ireland. Another population, nesting in Svalbard, winters on the Solway Firth in north-west England and

south-west Scotland. These birds migrate down the west coast of Norway then over the North Sea, before crossing overland over northern England and southern Scotland to reach the Solway. The third population breeds in northern Russia on Novaya Zemlya and Vaigach Island. These birds migrate through the White Sea, overland to the Gulf of Finland and then through the Baltic to their principal winter quarters in the Netherlands.

Since 1980 a fourth population has begun to nest on the Swedish island of Gotland and neighbouring islands in the middle of the Baltic Sea. It is believed that these birds originate from the Russian population and they also winter in the Netherlands.

The pattern of the Barnacle Goose's plumage is very distinctive and carries over long distances.

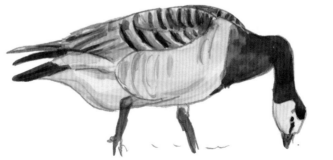

A pair of Barnacles with Pinkfeet. Barnacles associating with Pinkfeet are most likely to have originated from the population breeding in east Greenland - 14 November 2000.

Observations and ringing recoveries have shown that individuals from all four populations have been recorded in the region. Each year small numbers are seen on the grazing marshes or inland within the Pinkfeet flocks; more rarely small flocks have been noted on the coastal grazing marshes. The Barnacle Geese feeding with Pinkfeet are undoubtedly of Greenland origin and have become caught up with the Pinkfeet flocks in Greenland or during their migration stop-offs in Iceland.

Singles or small groups in October and November, seen passing along the coastline during on-shore northerly gales or subsequently among Brent or resting on the grazing marshes, most likely originate from the Svalbard breeding grounds and have been blown further south from their route, which normally takes them overland to the Solway. This belief has been strengthened by sightings of colour-ringed birds at Wells and Cley.

Small numbers and, more rarely, flocks which have appeared in mid or late winter are thought to have been forced to venture over the North Sea due to periods of severe winter weather in the Netherlands. Their occurrence frequently corresponds with the arrival of other continental birds and waterfowl. Again, this idea has been strengthened by the observation of colour-ringed

Barnacles and has even included a sighting of four individuals from a flock of six Barnacle Geese at Holkham, which originated from the new breeding population in Gotland.

Many of these colour-ringed birds have subsequently been seen back within their traditional ranges, showing that many geese have the ability to re-orientate themselves.

Small numbers of feral birds are to be found all year within the region and larger, free-flying flocks are present in other areas of the country. The presence of such flocks has led to some confusion as to the origins of regular sightings of small flocks of Barnacle Geese moving along the coast in May. It is possible that these movements could be some of the feral birds showing a spring migratory urge. However, several local observations of birds flying out to sea, calling, suggest that at least some of these are of wild stock, most probably birds from the Netherlands, re-orientating themselves before moving back towards the breeding grounds.

When lucky enough to encounter a small flock of Barnacles moving along the coast it is always surprising how an attractive flock of small-billed geese can produce such a loud, barking call. The noise of the flock can only be likened to a pack of small, yapping dogs.

Barnacle Geese at Holkham, part of a small influx. The occurence of such small flocks gives the opportunity to gain some experience of their behaviour, such as this threat posture. Here the closed wings are raised alternately clear of the body producing a flickering effect.

Bean Goose *Anser fabalis*

This goose appears in the area in two separate forms, the nominate race *A.f.fabalis*, known as the Taiga Bean Goose, and the sub-species *A.f.rossicus*, known as the Tundra Bean Goose. Of the two, the Tundra Bean Goose is by far the most regularly seen. Individuals or small numbers are often seen mixed in with the Pinkfeet flocks and readily move inland with them to feed on the sugar-beet tops. The occasional individual is also noted in amongst the White-fronted Geese. More rarely, small flocks have occurred in mid or late winter and, in common with other wildfowl, have crossed the North Sea during a cold snap in mainland Europe.

The Taiga Bean Goose is a much less frequent visitor. It prefers grazing marshes where it has been noted either on its own or in the loose company of Whitefronts and feral Greylag flocks. Although most often encountered singly or in pairs, there are a few records of small parties. It has only been recorded inland on sugar-beet tops with Pinkfeet on one occasion when a pair were briefly seen at Brancaster on 27 December 1999.

In contrast to the other geese which reach our shores, the nesting range of Bean Geese covers a huge, broad band from northern Scandinavia through the northern half of Russia to eastern-most Siberia. The Taiga and Tundra Bean Geese are the two western-most nesting of the five described forms. They differ further from the other geese in their surprising range of nesting habits. The ranges of the various forms overlap and merge in many areas so when describing typical nesting habitats and areas, we can only generalise.

Taiga Bean Goose

The Taiga Bean Goose nests in northern-most Scandinavia, through the northern half of Russia, eastwards towards the Ural mountains. It nests in a surprisingly wide range of habitats. In the southern half of its range it nests, uniquely, in thick coniferous forest. The climate causes the vegetation to change progressively from coniferous forest to willow and birch scrub as we travel further northwards. The geese in turn have to adapt their habits to the changing habitat. Some Taiga Bean Geese breeding in the northern extremes of their range nest in more tundra like habitat. The main wintering areas of this race are the Low Countries and central Europe. In addition there are two very small traditional wintering populations within the British Isles, which number only a few hundred birds. One is in the Yare Valley in east Norfolk and the other in the Carron Valley in Scotland. Both populations are small and faithful to their winter quarters and it is most likely that Taiga Bean Geese seen in north Norfolk belong to the population wintering in continental Europe.

A pair of Taiga Bean Geese at Stiffkey, January 1999. These two, recognisable by the white 'halters' around their bills, spent most of their time away from other geese or associated loosely with Greylags.

Tundra Bean Goose

The Tundra Bean Goose is more typical in its choice of open nesting areas and habitats, preferring high Arctic tundra areas of northern Russia and Siberia, from the Kanin Peninsula eastwards to the Taymyr Peninsula. Its wintering range is mainly concentrated in Sweden, Denmark, Germany, the Low Countries and France.

Field appearance and identification

Bean Geese are very similar in appearance to Pinkfeet (which were once regarded as a further sub-species of the Bean Goose). They differ in having the pale markings of their bill and legs bright orange-yellow. On a winter's day, with good lighting conditions, this bare-part colour makes identification fairly straightforward. However, the very nature of wild geese and winter weather frequently make identification more difficult. Distance and poor light can make colour interpretation impossible or, at least, unreliable. In such circumstances it is better to concentrate on the structure and profile of the head and bill while you wait and hope for the light to improve.

Typically Bean Geese are heavier-headed with a stronger wedge-shaped bill. The angular profile of the head and bill are, in some ways, reminiscent of an Eider, whereas Pinkfeet usually appear more round-headed with smaller, more delicate bills. Other pitfalls are young White-fronted Geese which lack the black belly bars and extensive white forehead of their parents but, in common with Bean Geese, have bright orange-yellow legs. Again, check the head shape and the markings of the back; young Whitefronts appear very dark and lack the pale frosty edges to the back feathers. Beware too of Pinkfeet in low winter sunshine which can sometimes make their legs appear quite orange; however, in such situations there is often a fleshy hue to them. The last cautionary note concerns the use of the darker forewing of Bean Geese compared to the pale grey of Pinkfeet as a distinctive field mark. This is stressed in many field guides and, in good light with prolonged views of the upper wing of these geese, it is indeed distinctive. Such conditions are rare however in the winter light of the north Norfolk landscape and fractionally different viewing angles can dramatically change the tone of the feathers.

A single Tundra Bean Goose (centre) with two Pinkfeet. The upper picture shows the geese in poor light. Here, the angular profile of the heavier head and bill are the best field marks to look for as you hope for the light to improve. As the sun breaks through, the yellow-orange colour on the legs and bill is instantly apparent (lower picture). Note also the darker, browner body feathers with their frosty-white edges.

This attitude towards the identification of Bean Geese is not intended to appear daunting or defeatist but, when dealing with species which can be difficult to assess, it is always better to lean towards caution, particularly if the light is poor or experience limited. Careful observation and patience will eventually reward the observer with good views and valuable experience of these potentially tricky geese.

Racial Identification

So, now we have found our Bean Goose, which race does it belong to? Again good light, viewing conditions and careful observation should make racial identification possible. However, you will sometimes come across individuals which do not fit comfortably into either category. Such individuals are best enjoyed simply as Bean Geese. Modern ornithology tends to fit the identification of birds into over-simplistic categories. However, looking through a flock of familiar geese such as Pinkfeet you will see a huge variation in size, shape and bill markings. It is not surprising then that some Bean Geese fall in between or outside the following descriptions. The Taiga Bean Goose is, on average, larger, longer-necked and has a proportionately longer bill than the Tundra Bean Goose. The bill markings of this race vary considerably from wholly orange, with a dark tip or 'nail', to those where the orange is reduced to a small band just behind the dark nail.

The Tundra Bean Goose is ,on average, more like a Pink-footed Goose in shape but has a heavier head and bill. It is slightly shorter-necked than the Taiga Bean Goose, giving it a more stocky appearance. The bill markings are less variable, with the majority of birds showing a black bill with just a small orange band towards the tip, just behind the nail.

Both races frequently show a small, white area of feathering around the base of the bill, sometimes referred to as a halter. This is a feature which is less frequently, but not uncommonly, seen in Pinkfeet.

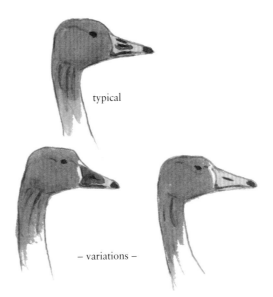

typical

– variations –

Taiga Bean Geese show a wide variation from typically marked birds to birds where the black markings are greatly reduced. Others show a Tundra-type bill marking.

Tundra Bean Geese are less variable in their bill markings, with the vast majority having just a small orange band towards the bill-tip.

Taiga Bean Geese also tend to have longer necks and bills than Tundra Bean Geese. You may observe birds that do not fit comfortably into either category; such individuals are best enjoyed simply as Bean Geese!

A drizzly day at Lady Anne's Drive sees a Red-breasted Goose which has been associating with local Brents, rubbing shoulders with the Whitefronts. These three species may not be complete strangers to each other as populations of each nest on the Taymyr Peninsular in Siberia - February 2000.

Waifs and strays and feral breeders

Bearing in mind the combined breeding ranges, migration routes and wintering areas of our main visiting geese, together with their gregarious habits, it is little wonder that wild geese of several other species have become mixed up with them and been seen within the area. We have already discussed the ways that Pale-bellied Brents and Black Brants have most probably ended up on our coast and in the following pages we will look at some of the other vagrants and the circumstances of their occurance. We shall briefly look at the feral populations of Greylags and Canada Geese and find out that both species have also occurred as wild vagrants. Another species, the Egyptian Goose, although more closely related to Shelducks, is also briefly looked at, as the region is the British stronghold for this species.

One of the biggest stumbling blocks when assessing the origins of unusual wildfowl is the possibility of escapes from wildfowl collections and the presence of feral populations. When faced with one of these 'waifs and strays', analysis of the conditions and circumstances of arrival, the host species it is associated with and the behaviour of the individual are strong pointers as to the likelihood of it being a genuine lost wild goose or an escape. For example, a timid Snow Goose, feeding and flighting out to roost each day with a large group of Pinkfeet, is more likely to be of wild origin than an approachable Snow Goose associating with feral Greylags. Pinkfeet would be a likely host species for a lost Snow goose in north Norfolk since some of the Pinkfeet use Greenland as a nesting and moulting area and some Snow Geese nest in north-west Greenland. Of course, unless a vagrant is colour-ringed or neck-collared within its natural range, you can never be 100 per cent sure but a little common sense and unbiased thought will help to make rational decisions and fuel the imagination as to how a vagrant may have ended up here.

These rarities are best treated as an unexpected bonus which enhances the goose-watching season. Goose-watching is about becoming familiar and involved with the routines, habits, patterns, spectacles and developments of the regular species.

A Greenland Whitefront, Barnacle and 'small' Canada Goose amongst the vast Pinkfeet flocks - 8 January 2000.

Lesser White-fronted Goose *Anser erythropus*

This is a very rare visitor to the region where genuine vagrants are most likely to be encountered in the latter half of the winter. The Lesser Whitefront breeds in a thin band from northern Scandinavia, eastwards through Russia, to eastern Siberia. Typical nesting areas include the edges of the northern taiga forests or amongst the patchy dwarf forests, rough grasses, bogs and rocky areas of the tundra. The main wintering areas are open country around the Caspian and Black Seas, eastwards to China.

The Scandinavian populations have declined dramatically during the latter half of the 1900s. Hunting pressures on the migration routes and wintering areas and human disturbance on the breeding grounds, in particular reindeer herders and their wild-living herds, are suggested reasons for this decline. Currently, there are several re-introduction schemes in Scandinavia using Barnacle Geese as foster parents. Some of these efforts have been successful as small numbers of Lesser Whitefronts now winter in the Netherlands.

A colour-ringed bird from a release scheme in Finnish Lapland has already been noted with Taiga Bean Geese in the Yare Valley in east Norfolk. The occurrence of such birds and the presence of unringed escaped birds which roam the country make records of Lesser Whitefronts very difficult to assess. However, three records of single adult birds with Whitefronts at Holkham in 1983, 1995 and 1997 are the best recent candidates as genuine wild vagrants. The latest two arrived with influxes of White-fronted Geese.

Lesser White-fronted Geese are on average smaller than White-fronted Geese. Structurally they are shorter-necked, with smaller rounded heads and smaller bills. The adult birds usually have more extensive white foreheads and less extensive black belly bars than their larger cousins. Young birds lack these plumage characteristics, however, at all ages, a bright yellow eye-ring is highly distinctive. White-fronted Geese occasionally show yellow eye-rings but never so large nor so vivid as Lessers do. They are also characteristic in their feeding action, compared to other species of grey geese they graze much faster and their progress through the flock seems double the speed.

Lesser White-fronted Goose with Whitefronts.

This Lesser White-fronted Goose (centre left) arrived with an influx of Whitefronts at Holkham. It constantly wandered between the other geese gesturing by flicking its head and continually calling, so was assumed to be a gander. This Tundra Bean Goose (centre right) also arrived during the same influx - 8 February 1997.

Greenland White-fronted Goose *Anser albifrons flavirostris*

Greenland Whitefronts are very rare in the region and are most usually seen in the company of Pinkfeet. Although regarded as a sub-species of the White-fronted Goose, its isolated breeding range has enabled its appearance and habits to evolve into a markedly different goose.

On a world scale, the Greenland Whitefront is a rare goose with a population of only around 12,000 birds. Western Greenland, as its name suggests, is the breeding ground. Here it breeds on lake-covered plateaux, favouring acid bogs and heathland. The entire population winters in the British Isles, mainly in Ireland and western Scotland, using Iceland as its stop-off point.
In north Norfolk it was first recorded in 1960 when a single was seen. Since then there have only been around a dozen records, mainly with Pinkfeet. The winter of 1999/2000 was exceptional, with at least six different individuals recorded. Records have involved both adult and young birds. Most birds are seen singly but pairs have occasionally been observed.

In good light, and at close range, separation from the White-fronted Goose is relatively straightforward. Greenland birds have a longer bill, which is orange-yellow compared to our Russian Whitefronts, which have a shorter flesh-coloured bill. This colour at longer range, particularly in the poor winter light, does not carry well and, also in certain lights, the pink bill of the Russian birds can appear orange. In such circumstances there are several other features which will help to clinch the correct identification.

The Greenland Whitefronts are heavier-headed and have longer, heavier bills than Russian Whitefronts. Their overall plumage, at all ages, is darker and shows less contrast between the belly and flank feathers. Furthermore, because the belly feathers are much darker, the black belly-bars of the adults are less contrasting. Greenland Whitefronts exhibit a tail pattern that is distinctive from Russian birds in that their tails are black with just a thin white border to the tip and sides. Russian birds have paler grey tails, with a broad white tip and border.

It is not unusual to see the occasional Russian Whitefront away from the grazing marshes at Holkham and feeding inland with Pinkfeet, so do not assume every White-fronted Goose with Pinkfeet is going to be a Greenland bird. Careful observation of structural and plumage features, particularly in poor light when colour may change or disappear, should enable correct identification or at least provide valuable experience.

Studies of a young Greenland Whitefront and an adult Russian Whitefront (centre) allow comparison of their different tail markings.

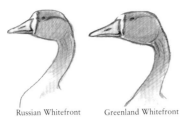

Russian Whitefront   Greenland Whitefront

The yellow-orange bills of Greenland birds are longer and heavier-based when compared to the pink bill of Russian birds. However, in the poor winter light, colour can be difficult to assess and these structural differences can be more useful as an aid to identification.

An adult Greenland Whitefront feeding on the outside edge of a Pinkfeet flock. This rare goose is found almost exclusively associating with large Pinkfeet flocks - 5 January 2001.

Red-breasted Goose *Branta ruficollis*

The first record of this beautiful small goose in the area was when a young bird appeared with Brent Geese at Stiffkey on the 10th November 1983. This bird caused quite a stir the following weekend when the flock it was in moved to Wells and a great crowd of birdwatchers lined the roadside to view it. At the time it was a very rare visitor to Britain and only the second individual to have been seen in the county, the first being back in 1962 in east Norfolk. In recent times large gatherings of birdwatchers have become a familiar sight following the discovery of a rarity; however, in the early 1980s this was quite a spectacle and local talking point. This bird remained in the local area all winter, ranging westwards as far as Holme, before returning eastwards and was finally seen bathing and preening near the whelksheds in Wells harbour on the 23rd March 1984.

Since then the occurrence of the Red-breasted Goose has become slightly more frequent, with a further half-dozen records. All have been in the company of Brents, with the exception of one, which somehow got mixed up with Pinkfeet. Locally this bird was first seen at Egmere on the 27th December 2000. It had previously been seen briefly

coming in to roost in Aberdeenshire one evening earlier in the winter but was not seen anymore until it was observed at Egmere. During its stay it was very difficult to see due to its small size and the sheer numbers of the larger Pinkfeet it associated with. Its faster feeding manner was comical to watch as it rapidly weaved its way through the flock. Its different appearance, and the fact that it was obviously lost, resulted in frequent threats and pokes from the Pinkfeet which, in turn led to fast evasive runs and flapping jumps forward. It was last seen at Brancaster on the 8th January 2001. During the last week of January 2001 it was back in Scotland, this time in the Loch Leven area. Red-breasted Geese breed in northern Siberia, with nearly the entire world population nesting on the Taymyr Peninsula. It winters near the Black and Caspian Seas, south to Greece and Turkey. On a world scale it is a rare goose, whose numbers have been in steady decline over the last century.

Studies of a young Red-breasted Goose at Wells-next-the-Sea. Adult birds have much larger red cheek-patches and only two white bars on the coverts.

Red-breasted Goose alighting with the Brents- 31 January 2001.

In north Norfolk they show a preference for grazing marshes and cereal fields. Birds arriving in early winter often associate with the first Brent flocks to have left the salt marshes and turned to grass and cereal. One young bird which arrived on the Wells saltings in late October 1994 moved onto winter wheat with a small Brent flock. It was so much more at home feeding here that one evening, as dusk approached, the flock ceased feeding and headed out over the salt marsh to roost on the shore; unexpectedly the Red-breast separated from the flock and dropped back onto the cereal.

Feeling alone it quickly took flight again and rapidly flew to catch up with the Brents. On the last morning of its stay, the 6th November 1994, this bird, along with its host flock of Brents, suddenly took off and headed east. There was a real purpose in their manner and there was no other explanation for their action than they had made the decision to move on. Later that day, by chance, the Red-breasted Goose, along with the Brent flock, was seen heading southwards over the sea at Winterton.

Red-breasted Goose alighting with the Brents - 31 January 2001.

Snow Goose *Anser caerulescens*

The Snow Goose has been recorded on a few occasions as a wild vagrant; the most recent records are of singles within the large Pinkfeet flocks. Snow Geese breed in north-west Greenland, westwards across the whole of arctic North America to the extreme north-east of Siberia. They occur in two races; the nominate race, *A.c.caerulescens* breeds over much of the range, and being the smaller of the two races is referred to as the Lesser Snow Goose. The larger form, *A.c.atlanticus*, the Greater Snow Goose, has a more restricted range, nesting on islands surrounding Baffin Bay, in north-east Canada and north-west Greenland.

The Snow Goose occurs in two different colour forms, one all white with black wing-tips, the other largely grey-brown with a white head and neck. The back feathers of this darker form often have a bluish cast and have resulted in this form being referred to as the Blue Goose. Because of its very different appearance, the Blue Goose was once thought to be a separate species.

Although the two colour-forms prefer mates of the same appearance, some mixed pairs exist and intermediate coloured birds are recorded. Interestingly blue forms are common in Lessers but very rare in Greaters. Young birds differ from adults in that their white feathers are smudged with grey-brown and the reddish bill of their parents is replaced with grey. Assigning a vagrant Snow Goose to either population is difficult without a good knowledge of the species and its variations in size and shape. The Snow Goose is commonly kept in wildfowl collections and small feral breeding colonies have become established, clouding the true status of birds seen in the wild.

Three recent records, however, were undoubtedly wild birds and all involved white adults with Pinkfeet. The first was seen at Wells flighting with Pinkfeet from the roost site on the 18th February 1984. Another stayed with the Pinkfeet in north-west Norfolk from the 17th November 1985 to the 14th January 1986. The third was present again in north and north-west Norfolk, mainly in the Brancaster area, from the 6th December 1996 to at least the 25th February 1997. This individual was also seen with Pinkfeet in Lancashire both before and after its stay in north Norfolk. Evidence of the ability of wild Snow Geese to reach Europe was confirmed when a Lesser Snow Goose, carrying colour rings, in the company of seventeen other Snow Geese, was seen in the Netherlands and was originally ringed at La Perouse Bay, 40km east of Churchill, Manitoba in Canada.

A Snow Goose coming off the roost at Wells with thousands of Pinkfeet, 18 February, 1984.

Canada Goose *Branta canadensis*

This familiar goose was first introduced into Norfolk in the seventeenth century. Feral flocks, descendants of these released birds, are regularly encountered throughout north Norfolk, being more common in the west of the region.

The Canada Goose is a native of North America where it breeds throughout Canada, Alaska and in some north-central states of the USA. The bulk of the population is migratory and winters in the USA. Around eleven separate forms are recognised of which the nominate race, the Atlantic Canada Goose, *B.c.canadensis*, is the form to which the feral flocks breeding in the British Isles belong. The races vary dramatically in size from the largest, the Giant Canada Goose, which is bigger still than our feral birds, through to the tiny short-necked Cackling Goose, which is smaller than a Brent Goose.

In north Norfolk around half a dozen of the smaller races have occurred as genuine wild vagrants amongst the Pinkfeet. The appearance of the races of Canada Geese is relatively complex and at present poorly documented. The birds of north Norfolk have shown distinct characteristics and current information has helped to form the suspicion that these birds are most likely to be one of the following three races: Richardson's Goose *B.c.hutchinsii*, Lesser Canada Goose *B.c.parvipes*, or Todd's Canada Goose *B.c.interior*.

Not surprisingly, these are amongst the most northern and eastern of the North American races; all are long distance migrants and amongst the most likely forms to occur as wild vagrants.

Geographically, Pinkfeet are the obvious host species to bring a wild Canada Goose to north Norfolk. Interestingly, but not that surprisingly, the same large Pinkfeet flocks which have contained these smaller forms of Canada Geese have also played host to Greenland Whitefronts and Barnacle Geese.

Field impressions of the smaller races of Canada Goose that have been observed amongst the Pinkfeet in north Norfolk.

The Canada Goose races are very complex and poorly documented. The true identity ot these rare stragglers may never be proven. Current literature suggests that these birds fall into one of the following categories: (left) **Todd's Canada Goose**; slightly bulkier than Pinkfeet with a curious 'snakey neck' when feeding. When alert, stands taller than Pinkfeet; (middle) a pair of **Lesser Canada Geese**; Pink-footed sized versions of the large, familiar feral birds in every respect; (right) the Brent Goose-sized **Richardson's Goose**; dainty, short-necked and small-billed. This bird was uniformly dark above and below with a white band dividing its black neck from its dark breast, a very beautiful goose.

This picture was made from field sketches and paintings and only serves to show a basic impression. The actual individuals were seen at the following places: **Todd's Canada Goose**, adult Brancaster, December 1999; first-winter Wells area, January 2000; **Lesser Canada Goose**, pair Houghton, January 1999; **Richardson's Goose**, Holkham, February 1999.

A Richardson's Canada Goose and Barnacle pair with Pinkfeet. This attractive small race of Canada Goose is between a Brent and Pink-footed Goose in size. 13 February 1999.

A pair of Lesser Canada Geese amidst a large group of Pinkfeet. These birds are essentially Pink-footed Goose sized versions of the familiar feral Canada Geese in both colour and structure - 8 January 1999.

Greylag Goose *Anser anser*

The Greylag is a familiar bird of the region throughout the year. This feral population stems from introductions from the Hebrides, which contain some of the strongholds of the native wild British population. Back in history, Greylags almost certainly occurred locally in a natural wild state. The history of these current feral flocks can be traced back to the 1930s, with some of the first birds being released on Holkham Lake. Holkham Lake has become a local stronghold and an important moulting ground for Greylags within the county. Greylags are found throughout the region and nest in many areas close to water. During the winter months, flocks of up to 800 can be seen, often feeding on stubble fields, grazing marshes, parkland and also sugar-beet close to the coast.

The Greylag has a fragmented breeding range right across Europe, Russia and Siberia. In the past it would have nested throughout this area but pressures due to over-hunting and land drainage have resulted in its range becoming fragmented. Iceland also holds a large breeding population. Icelandic birds winter mainly in Scotland, Continental European birds winter in southern Europe and North Africa, while birds from Russia and Siberia winter from the Black Sea eastwards through India to eastern China.

In north Norfolk the Greylag almost certainly occurs as a wild vagrant; however, due to the existence of feral flocks both here and in Europe, it is difficult to be certain of a stray bird's origin.

Occasional ones and twos, keeping with the Pinkfeet, are likely to be of Icelandic origin, while individuals or small parties moving over the sea or arriving after cold weather could be of wild European or Russian stock.

Large feral populations of Greylags are resident in north Norfolk, however wild stragglers are occasionally encountered in winter.

Egyptian Goose *Alopochen aegyptiacus*

Although referred to as a goose, this species is more closely related to Shelducks. It was introduced into Britain around the end of the seventeenth century and by the end of the nineteenth was firmly established in Norfolk. North Norfolk, in particular Holkham Park, is now regarded as the stronghold of the British population. Due to this feral population's ability to sustain itself over such a long period it was placed on the official list of British birds in 1971.

It is an extremely early nester, with pairs displaying and becoming territorial in the early autumn. Breeding territories are forcefully defended and the pair may even have eggs by the end of December. The nest is constructed or situated high up in trees, usually in a hole, in large tree-forks or on a broken limb. In Holkham Park mature beech trees are favoured, since they are prone to disease and their large trunks and branches become hollow and weak. These are soon damaged by storms and make ideal nesting places. The nest is most often near water but occasionally it may be over half a mile away.

Once all the eggs have hatched, the parents call to their young to encourage them to jump down, then gather them together and lead them to the safety of water. Great clouds of grey down cover nearby branches and the ground below the nest following the departure of the young. The first young are frequently seen in late January or early February at a time when large numbers of wild geese are still present. The Egyptian Goose is essentially an African species which occurs throughout the continent where fresh water is found. In Egypt it was formally a numerous species whose numbers have dwindled greatly during the last century.

Young Egyptian Geese can be seen as early as January - the heart of the wild goose season.

An unusual hybrid

This individual was first seen on 7th January 1997 amongst the Whitefronts at Holkham, apparently paired to a Barnacle Goose. It was shortly afterwards noted within the Pinkfeet flocks and since then it has become very much a feature of the winter Pinkfeet flocks. It is a hybrid goose whose parentage is uncertain but, almost certainly, one of its parents was a Barnacle Goose. The appearance of hybrids is often uncertain or poorly documented. The plumage and pale leg colour does show elements of a blue phase Snow Goose, which its other parent may be. Its origins are of course uncertain but it is as likely to be a wild hybrid as it is to be an escape.

Whatever its origins, this goose obviously migrates with the Pinkfeet back to their breeding grounds in either Iceland or Greenland and its attractive appearance has helped to illustrate the interchange of feeding areas and roost sites of Pinkfeet within the area. It has also helped to indicate the movements of Pinkfeet from the breeding areas to north Norfolk by its occurance at other traditional Pinkfeet sites in the British Isles.

In the first two winters it was seen here it was paired to a Barnacle, however, in the following years, it has returned alone.

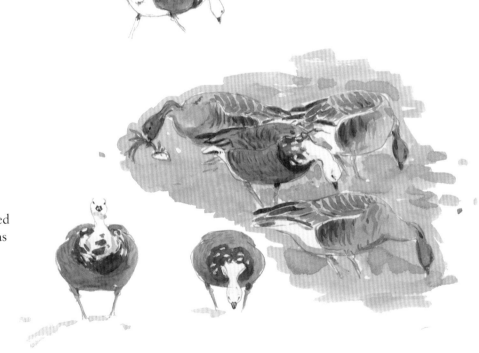

Watching wild geese and fieldcraft

Wild geese are, on the whole, very shy birds, suspicious of man and his activities. Anyone watching a group of Pinkfeet feeding close to the busy car park at Lady Anne's Drive, which leads to Holkham beach may find this hard to believe. However, the same flock, feeding only half a mile inland, behaves totally differently. This is a perfect example of the fickleness and long memories of wild geese. Areas such as Lady Anne's Drive have, over several years, become known to geese as a safe feeding area and the droves of cars and people, separated by a fence pose no threat to them.

In other areas, such as inland sugar-beet fields the very same geese are extremely wary. This is because, in these areas, they may be actively discouraged from certain fields by farmers and farm workers or by nearby shooting, which will make them very edgy.

In such situations, if you so much as open a car door the whole flock will take to the wing. This causes disturbance to their feeding and friction with farmers. Many farms are quite happy to have Pinkfeet feeding on sugar-beet tops. However, any disturbance may send them on to a neighbouring field of cereal, which will not be tolerated. This will cause extra work for the farm and bad feeling towards birdwatchers. Using your car as a hide to watch from is the best tactic, as geese are less wary of cars. Diesel engines are more prone to disturb geese as they recognise the engine noise and associate it with farm vehicles. Common sense, such as not wearing striking clothing and avoiding breaking the horizon or standing in open areas such as gaps in hedges or gates, will greatly reduce the risk of flushing them.

Respect for feeding geese and other users of the road and countryside, combined with the use of fieldcraft, should reduce local friction, reduce unnecessary disturbance and ultimately provide better opportunities to watch and learn about wild geese.

Alert Whitefronts shortly before taking flight - 13 February 1999.

Equipment

Obviously good-quality, warm, weatherproof clothing and footwear are essential for long periods of sitting still watching geese in winter weather. To observe geese, binoculars 8x or 10x are essential. A telescope for long range geese is invaluable. Personally, I prefer a 20x wide-angle eyepiece, as I find it possible to identify geese and also the wide-angle makes observation of groups and behaviour possible. Other observers prefer 30x wide-angle lenses or zoom lenses, which bring the birds even closer; however the field of view will be smaller. Telescopes are best used with a tripod or a car window mount. A notebook, pens and pencils are very useful as observations and details can be recorded instantly rather than having to rely on memory.

Sketching

Drawing is a good way to learn about the appearance and behaviour of geese as it focuses your attention for long periods. At times it can be frustrating as the geese are constantly on the move and the weather and light continually changing. It is worth persevering for you will soon find another goose in the same position that will enable you to finish your drawing. Before long, characteristic stances and behaviour become more evident and it is surprising how quickly elements of behaviour become familiar. With more practice and experience, confidence will grow and these will become evident in the drawing. Expect to make lots of mistakes for this is one of the key elements of learning. When a sketch goes wrong, forget about it and start another; playing around with a bad drawing will not make it a good one. I have always found that drawing is far more enjoyable if you don't worry about what people think and don't set out with the idea of creating a great work of art. These drawings are primarily for yourself and a tool for learning, in this instance, about wild geese.

You don't need to spend a fortune on art equipment to build up a basic collection of materials which will serve you well for drawing and painting outdoors. All the drawings and virtually all the paintings in this book are painted outdoors from life using art equipment and materials which are stored in a small rucksack and kept to the minimum weight possible. My basic painting kit comprises a small plastic box containing paints, a small plastic water pot, a rubber, clips to stop paper flapping in the wind, an A4 wire-bound sketchbook (wire-bound to stop paper coming detached) a small folder containing various sizes of watercolour paper (140lb) cut up from large sheets, two sections of plastic pipe sealed at one end, one for paintbrushes and the other for pencils. The addition of a small piece of foam or polystyrene placed in the bottom of the pencil tube should prevent damage to their tips. Finally, a small piece of foam matting or a small fold-up stool to sit on is useful. Soft lead pencils 2B-4B, kept sharp, enable fast smooth lines and greater speed to react to movement. I find student quality watercolours fine for painting and considerably cheaper than artist-quality ones. I use tubes whereas many prefer pans of colour, either are fine and the colour can be mixed on the white lid of the plastic box.

My basic colours for winter geese are cobalt blue, light red, yellow ochre and lemon yellow. With these paints it is possible to mix up all the colours I need. It is worth investing in good quality brushes, sable, or at least sable mix. These will hold their shape much longer and consistently allow quick accurate strokes. Despite their greater cost they will last much longer than cheaper alternatives. Pointed brushes, a No.6, a No.8 and a No.10 are a good selection to have.

Threats and predators

Thick Fog
Thick fog can be a serious hazard for geese, particularly Pinkfeet which travel over large distances to feed. The sudden appearance of thick fog in the morning can cause huge problems for Pinkfeet leaving their roosts for as they rise above the fog layer and away from the voices of the hordes below they soon become disorientated and lost. Lost groups can be heard flying around above the fog for hours until they find a clear patch or their calls are finally answered from below to help guide them down. Not surprisingly, a distinct panic can be detected in the calls of these lost and disorientated flocks.

Barnacle Geese

More serious is the sudden appearance, during the day, of a thick fog-bank, developing or moving in from the sea, over the coast and inland. Now this is a really dangerous time for Pinkfeet for, in these circumstances, the whole winter population from all the roost sites is caught out feeding inland so there will not even be voices below the fog to guide them down to safety. The landscape quickly becomes dark and featureless as the evening progresses and dusk approaches. On such nights the geese can only fly around and around through the night waiting for returned calls or the fog to thin. Panic and confusion is very evident in their cries. During such nights their voices have been heard tens of miles out of their normal ranges due to their desperation to find somewhere to rest. One such terrible event happened on the night of the 13th November 1995.

Fog and Pinkfeet 13th November 1995

The worst recorded example of Pinkfeet becoming lost and disorientated in thick fog began on 13th November 1995 and continued throughout the night until the following morning. The preceding days had seen a typical pattern of moonlight feeding, with Pinkfeet feeding deep inland on sugar-beet tops by day, flighting out to their roosts, then returning back to their feeding fields by moonlight. During the late afternoon and early evening of the 13th, the whole coast and countryside were engulfed in thick fog. Pinkfeet became instantly lost as they attempted to head out to roost and the frantic calls of numerous Pinkfeet skeins could be heard flying round and round above the thick blanket of fog. Flocks, in their desperation to find land, were attracted to the glow of street lamps below and large numbers were recorded landing in bizarre locations such as the Fakenham bypass, the floodlit car park of

Pink-footed Goose

English Country Cottages in Sculthorpe village and a small paddock in the middle of Binham, among other places. As the night drew on, the voices, distinctly panic stricken and weary, were beginning to be heard in locations which, at that time, were way out of their normal range, with flocks calling above Cromer, Sheringham, Holt and Dereham. Calls could be heard throughout the night until the following morning, when improved visibility eventually enabled them to reorientate themselves, rest and recover from this trauma and their exhaustion.

Predators

Winter geese suffer little natural predation on their winter quarters. This may be due to their large numbers and constant lookouts. Their roost-sites on water or vast inaccessible sands and mudflats give them maximum possible protection from ground predators such as foxes, who will be quick to prey on sick, injured or wounded geese who may be unable to move with the main flocks and are therefore weak and naturally vulnerable.

Geese are very wary of large birds of prey such as Peregrines and wandering Rough-legged or Common Buzzards. In north Norfolk these are no threat to the geese, although a friend of mine once saw a Peregrine take a Brent Goose.

The appearance of such a bird will frequently end in whole flocks of geese and other birds taking flight. This is a natural reaction provoked by both instinct and real experiences which geese face nearer their breeding sites from fearsome predators such as the large Gyr falcons and Sea Eagles. On the few rare occasions when Sea Eagles have wandered over this coast the reaction of geese, and for that matter all birds, is one of complete panic.

Aircraft, particularly propeller-driven planes and helicopters, produce the same panic since the appearance of their distant shapes in the sky and leisurely progress can produce a similar impression to a large aerial predator. Large kites and microlites cause similar unrest. The sudden appearance and noise of low- flying jets causes shock to everyone but the progress of high-flying passenger jets causes little panic. Their progress however is noted with interest and caution.

Pinkfeet, heads one side watching a jet aeroplane passing high overhead.

The real threat to wild geese is from man and his activities. Serious declines of species have been attributed to land drainage, changes in land use and over-exploitation in the form of over-hunting and egg collecting. In north Norfolk the real threats come from the way we use the land which, combined with safety of roost sites is ultimately the main reason that geese choose this particular area to spend their winter.

Wildfowling is essentially policed by its own members through bag limits and shooting-free zones, such as the actual roost sites. Wildfowling where geese are concerned is, in modern times, more about personal ethics rather than the need to provide food to feed families and its effects in north Norfolk have had little impact on the spectacular comeback of the Pinkfeet. Changes in agriculture or management of the land hold the key to the attractiveness, growth and development of this area to wild geese. For example, changes in livestock farming govern the amount and quality of grazing marshes, which are essential to all geese during some stage of their stay here. However, too much intensive mowing of grazing marshes makes large areas less attractive for the Whitefronts who seem to prefer rougher grazing marshes.

Pink-footed Goose

Recent proposals to reduce greatly sugar-beet production within the whole of Europe could prove very serious to the future of the Pinkfeet population in north Norfolk. Food availability during the winter is one of the essential requirements to enable such geese populations to continue to thrive. It seems that even the vast armies of wild geese whose great migrations, seasonal appearances and routines have come to be a sight of wonder, imagination and a symbol of the forces and rhythms of the natural world, are ultimately at our mercy.

A WILD GOOSE STORM DISASTER

Soon after dawn on the morning of January 3rd 1978 a violent storm crossed East Anglia. In its wake 140 wild geese lay dead in fields, along hedgerows and on the road. These were mainly Pinkfeet but included Canada, Greylag, 2 Brent and one Bean Goose. The following account of events leading to this avian disaster and the conclusions reached, have been compiled after examining available meteorological and ornithological data.

Over Norwich and east Norfolk the morning of January 3rd dawned bright and breezy, but in the west of the county storm clouds rolled out of the darkened western sky, towering above The Wash towards Lincolnshire. This was not an isolated build-up of cloud but a line of many active storm centres joined along a vigorous and extremely mobile cold front. This marked the boundary between warm moist air, which had lain over East Anglia over night and cold polar air rushing south-east across Britain from the north-west Atlantic. Temperatures dropped from 8degrees centigrade in the warm air to 2 degrees centigrade behind the front. Over northern Britain this frontal boundary was relatively inactive but approaching East Anglia it rapidly intensified as a renewed surge of cold air displaced more and more warm air upwards through the atmosphere (Fig. 1). This whole frontal airmass became completely unstable, resulting in the formation of numerous cumulonimbus or 'thunderstorm' clouds. Worse was to come.

When air is forced to rise very rapidly a localised spinning motion may be induced. The atmospheric forces acting on the rising air are identical to those which produce small whirlpools in the bath as water rushes down the plughole.

In the atmosphere such spinning columns are called dust devils, whirlwinds or tornadoes, depending on size. In Britain the largest are normally only a few tens of metres in diameter and last for just a few minutes. In America, large tornadoes may persist for up to an hour and cause severe damage along a trail half a kilometre wide.

On the morning of January 3rd the cold air surging across East Anglia at nearly 50mph caused sustained uplift of warm air. This produced vigorous upcurrents and several whirlwinds and small tornadoes were reported. The first was in Hull just before dawn and 2 hours later a larger tornado struck the Newmarket area inflicting considerable damage to houses, cars and a railway signal box. (Chorley L.G., *Meteorological Magazine*, No.1275, Vol. 107, Oct. 1978). Aubrey Buxton writing in the *NARVOS Report for 1978* states that Michael Hunt, the senior forecaster with Anglia TV, was informed by Dr. Meaden, Director of the Tornado Research Organisation, 'that at least 5 tornadoes were reported over northern East Anglia on the morning of January 3rd and considers that further unreported tornadoes were more than likely'. Hence it is probably reasonable to assume that, although no major tornadoes were sighted over The Wash or NW Norfolk, small tornadoes or funnel clouds could have developed. (A funnel cloud is a column of spinning air below a cumulonimbus cloud, but it does not reach the ground. Friction near the earth's surface breaks up the spinning motion).

The scene now changes to the salt-marshes surrounding The Wash, or possibly a field in Lincolnshire. A flock of wild geese is grazing or perhaps, as dawn breaks, they are flighting around The Wash between roosting and feeding areas.

Out of the dark western sky the storm approaches, heavy rain and sleet lash down, thunder and lightning reverberate across the sky, hailstones crash around and the squalls reach 50-60 mph. There is panic. Many geese fly east, running before the storm, trying to escape its fury.

Suddenly geese are sucked aloft like toy balloons. Caught in a whirling tornado their lungs are decompressed by the explosive drop in atmospheric pressure. Up, up they go. To what altitude is unknown but gliders accidentally caught in tornado clouds have been reported as experiencing uncontrollable uplift of over 10,000 ft! For a lightweight goose it could be much more.

The largest concentration of dead geese (105) was found between Castle Acre and Great Massingham, with Dereham 2, near Gressenhall 4 (including a Bean Goose), Wendling 14, Carlton Forehoe 3, Hethersett 10, Swardeston1 and Mattishall 1 (Fig. 2).

By the time the Mattishall bird was reported it had been cooked and eaten! Four birds were sent by Aubrey Buxton for post mortem examination (*NARVOS Report for 1978*). All four had ruptured livers and haemorrhaging, the result of blast, precussion or de-compression. This, it is reported, would alone have been enough to cause death but each one also had extensive internal injuries and bone damage, indicating that they had crashed to earth from a considerable height.

The birds picked up dead were found along a relatively narrow corridor between Castle Acre and Swardesrton. When extended north-west this corridor crosses southern parts of the Wash, the Welland estuary and into Nottinghamshire, passing close to Sleaford and Newark (Fig. 3). It is highly probable therefore, that the birds involved in this accident were feeding on the salt-marshes or mud-flats along the southern shores of the Wash, perhaps part of the Snettisham flock which is known to feed extensively between Snettisham and Nene mouth near Sutton Bridge and whose numbers declined that day from over 4500 to about 500. Four of the Canada Geese recovered carried B.T.O rings. All four had been ringed near Worksop, Notts, in 1970, 1971 and 1976 (two), and speculation arose that they could have been picked up by the storms over Nottinghamshire. This is possible but seems unlikely for three reasons: the large number of Pinkfeet involved (there are few records of large concentrations in Notts); no reports of dead geese in Lincolnshire; and most important, the storms had passed the Worksop/Nottingham area before reaching maximum intensity.

It is therefore concluded that the most likely sequence of events was that a flock of geese flighting the southern perimeter of The Wash at dawn, or panicked into the air by the approaching storm, was overtaken by a tornado or funnel cloud and forcibly sucked upwards to a considerable altitude, which caused death or unconsciousness. Their involuntary return to earth was then only a matter of time and occurred along a 30 mile path from near Castle Acre to just south of Norwich.
Footnote: Later that day observers at East Tuddenham, Costessey and Reepham reported skeins of geese numbering from 2 to 35 flying in a northwesterly direction, presumably finding their way 'home'.

Wally Thrower
Norfolk Bird and Mammal Report 1979

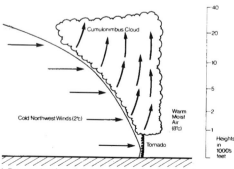

Fig.1 Cross-section through the frontal zone illustrating how the surge of cold air displaces the warm moist air. Cumulonimbus clouds are formed providing the air is unstable.

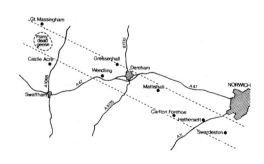

Fig.2 Corridor along which the dead geese were located.

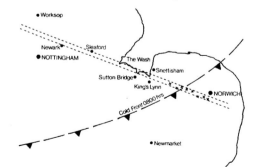

Fig.3 The projection of the "kill corridor" northwestwards across the southern boundary of The Wash and into Nottinghamshire. A cross is plotted in each area where dead geese were located.

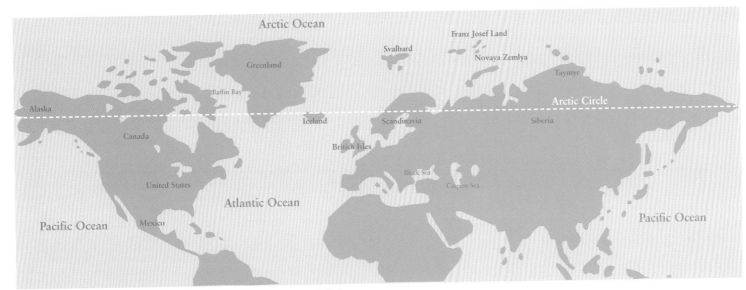

The combined breeding ranges of the geese recorded in north Norfolk forms a
continuous band around the Arctic.

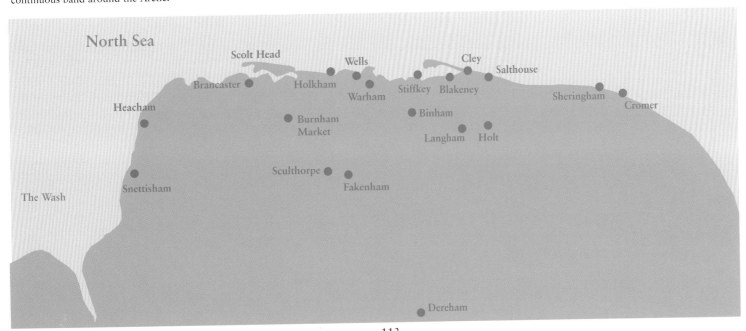

Bibliography

Cramp (1977) *The Birds of the Western Palearctic* Vol.1, Oxford University Press

Seago (1999) *The Birds of Norfolk*, Pica Press

Norfolk Bird and Mammal Report, 1953-2000

Bloomfield (1993) *Birds of the Holkham Area*

McCallum (1999) *North Norfolk Wildlife Through the Seasons*, Arlequin Press

British Trust for Ornithology, *Wetland Bird Surveys & The Wildfowl and Wader Counts*

Lorenz (1979) *The Year of The Greylag Goose*, Eyre Methuen

The Netherlands - Institute for Forestry and Nature Research (IBN-DLO), *Onze Rotgans in Siberia*

USEFUL GUIDES DEPICTING GEESE AND WILDFOWL

Scott (1961) *A Coloured Key to Wildfowl of the World*, Wildfowl and Wetlands Trust

Ogilvie (1998) *Photographic Handbook of the Wildfowl of the World*, New Holland

Madge & Burn (1987) *Wildfowl - an identification guide to ducks, geese and swans of the world*, Christopher Helm

GENERAL FIELD GUIDES TO BIRDS

Svensson & Grant (1999) *Collins Bird Guide*, Harper Collins

Jonsson (1992) *Birds of Europe*, Christopher Helm

SELECTED READING

Peter Scott (1936) *Morning Flight*, Country Life Limited

Peter Scott (1938) *Wild Chorus*, Country Life Limited

W.H. Hudson (1923) *Adventures Among Birds*, J.M. Dent & Son Limited

Pat Crinkle *Salt Marsh and Sand Dunes, Recollections of a Wildfowler and Naturalist*, Wells and District Wildfowlers Club.

Riviere (1930) *A History of the Birds of Norfolk*, Witherby

Stevenson (1866-90) John Van Voorst and Gurney and Jackson, *The Birds of Norfolk* Vol **1-3**

Acknowledgements

Thanks firstly to Andrew Bloomfield for many shared hours spent watching geese, for keeping me up to date with goose matters from his own observations and findings and also for his help and enthusiasm for this project

John Walters who transformed my rough ideas into the finished design of this book and actively encouraged its development from the early idea stages. To John Busby, Robert Gillmor and David Measures for their continued encouragement and help in this long process of learning to draw, paint and study wild creatures outdoors in their natural habitat. Further thanks to Robert for kindly agreeing to write the foreword.

To Natasha Drury for doing the typing, and to Roger and Margot Brownsword for commenting on the text.

Also to John Kemp, Carl Donner and Arthur Jenkins who have passed on some of their long experience of watching geese in the area and whose chance meetings are enthusiastic and frequently in good humour and have become very much a part of the local goose watching season.

This also gives me the chance to thank my family and friends and the numerous individuals who have helped in many different ways.

It would be impossible to complete these acknowledgements without mentioning the following artists whose outdoor drawings, paintings and observations, although frequently not related to geese, have given me much inspiration during the making of my own geese pictures. John Busby, Eric Ennion, Robert Hainard, Lars Jonsson, Bruno Liljefors, David Measures, Peter Scott's early works, Frank Southgate and John Walters.

More recently I have become greatly enthused by natural history writers such as Henry Williamson and R.B. Lockley.

Also the work of scientists, field naturalists and bird watchers such as Eric Ennion, Konrad Lorenz, Desmond Nethersole-Thompson, Niko Tinbergen and D.I.M Wallace. Their enthusiasm and passion for their subject comes through in their writing but not only this they have the ability to put over large amounts of detailed facts and information in a manner that is enjoyable to read and easy to digest.